Contemplative Aging
A Way of Being in Later Life

Contemplative Aging
A Way of Being in Later Life

by

Edmund Sherman, Ph.D.

Gordian Knot Books
An Imprint of Richard Altschuler & Associates, Inc.
New York

 For information contact the publisher, Richard Altschuler & Associates, Inc., at 100 West 57th Street, New York, NY 10019, RAltschuler@rcn.com or (212) 397-7233.

To correspond with the author directly send an email to Shermans2@verizon.net

Library of Congress Control Number: 2010924481
CIP data for this book are available from the Library of Congress

ISBN-13: 978-1-884092-99-2
ISBN-10: 1-884092-99-3

Gordian Knot Books is an imprint of
Richard Altschuler & Associates, Inc.

Cover Design and Layout: Josh Garfield

Printed in the United States of America

Dedication

To Arleen

Acknowledgements

There are several people who deserve special thanks for their help and support in the course of my writing this book. First I want to thank Theodore (Ted) Webb and Max Siporin, wise old friends and elders, who thoughtfully read and critiqued major parts of the book. Their contributions were constructive throughout. Another person deserving thanks is Mark Greenwold, whose artistic creativity and remarkable psychological growth in his later years provided reassurance and confirmation for me of the positive personal development that can occur in the second half of life.

Most important in this endeavor has been my wife, Arleen. Her love and very being were essential to its completion.

Finally it needs to be said that this is a highly derivative book, as the numerous quotes from persons ancient to modern and West to East will attest. Without their wise observations and insights this work would not have been possible. For what they have contributed to the substance of this book and to me personally in my later years they have my everlasting gratitude.

Contents

Introduction

What does the study of aging and old age, known as the science of gerontology, tell us about how we should spend the later years of our lives? The answer, paradoxically, is a great deal and not much. It tells us a great deal about elders *in general*, i.e., in the aggregate, based on averages from samples, but much less about elders *in particular*, i.e., as individuals who are never really average in every respect, including how to spend those later years of life. Gerontology is generally defined as the comprehensive study of aging and the problems of the aged. It is comprehensive in that it covers the aging process from birth to death, unlike geriatrics, which is the branch of medicine that deals only with the treatment of the physical problems of old age. There are certainly medical problems galore in old age, so physicians and nurses are members of the Gerontological Society of America, but so are sociologists, psychologists, psychiatrists, social workers, anthropologists, economists, and a host of people from other disciplines, such as history, philosophy, literature, and the arts in general. As the foremost organization for the study of aging and old age, it has to be comprehensive, as this array of disciplines indicates. All of this is simply to indicate the range and variety of disciplines providing us with information that might enable us to know better how to live out our later years.

As a gerontologist who has engaged in research, teaching, and practice in the field of aging, and as an octogenarian who has personally experienced some of the problems and issues of old age, I have something of a dual perspective on the subject. Consequently this book is written from both a professional and a personal perspective, and some of it is necessarily written in the first person.

Although there are many competing theories of aging in the field, there have been two rather encompassing theoretical orientations toward late life that tell us something about how it can or should be lived. The first of these is what has been called "activity" theory. It claims that the optimal pattern of aging is exemplified by the older person who maintains the activities of middle age as long as possible, and who finds substitutes for work when forced to retire, and who finds replacements for the inevitable loss of friends and loved ones. Although decreased socialization tends to be a fact in old age, from this theoretical perspective the decrease happens against the wishes of most older men and women. It is the withdrawal by society, rather than by the individual, that is held primarily responsible for decreased socialization.

Contrary to this is the view that decreased social interaction is a process of mutual disengagement, in which both society and the individual withdraw from each other in a natural kind of reciprocity. According to "disengagement" theory, society needs to provide opportunities for younger persons to assume the economic, familial, and civic roles and responsibilities that their elders have performed. Society needs this replenishment of youth for its own continuity and growth. Elders recognize this societal need as well as their own diminishing strength and capacity to function optimally in their former social roles. They also feel the need for some degree of withdrawal, to conserve their waning physical powers.

Now this sort of theory is anathema to many older persons who feel vigorous and highly capable well into their seventies and even eighties. I am reminded of a former colleague whose ninety-two-year-old father was still a practicing pediatrician, driving his car to and from clinics and hospitals because "he couldn't let up." He had been widowed for a number of years and lived alone in a distant city, without the requisite cooking and household skills to care for himself (in my colleague's estimation), so she tried to convince him to retire and move closer to her. His response was "Retire! What would I do with myself, if I retire?" She suggested that, instead of continuing to actively practice medicine, he could write a book about it based on his many years of experience. His response to that was, "Write about it! I've written four books and dozens of articles on pediatrics, and who reads them anymore? No thanks! I have to keep on the go."

We all know Type A personalities similar to this gentleman. They are activity personified, so activity theory suits them fine. In fact, people in their seventies, eighties, and even nineties are healthier and more vigorous in general than elders in the past, because of better nutrition and medical care. Individuals in the baby boom generation who are moving into elderhood seem to see themselves quite differently from earlier generations of elders. They tend to see themselves as a generation that will be more active and engaged productively in society much later into their lives. They not only see retirement coming later in their lives by choice, but also by necessity, with the likelihood of Social Security eligibility coming at a later age, and with the continuing loss of other pension options in the economy. Overall, in terms of this generalization, they certainly seem to fit the activity much more than the disengagement pattern.

Even before the arrival of the baby boomers on the gerontological scene, there was a general disengagement from disengagement theory among many thinkers in the field of aging. It appeared too much at odds with findings of better health and well being among active elders, and it appeared to portray them as too passive and withdrawing in a society that views itself as more proactive and achievement-oriented. Recently, in fact, it has been suggested (Tornstam, 2005) that there have been mismatches between theory and a number of empirical findings that imply underlying mid-life values about activity patterns that contemporary researchers often unwittingly project onto old age. These patterns are then seen by some gerontologists as evidence of successful aging. Indeed, the concept of successful aging has been used extensively in gerontology for quite some time. Within this concept there may be an image of a successful middle-class, middle-aged person whose qualities of activity, sociability, productivity, efficiency, health and wealth stand out. Even scholars in the field may unconsciously project these mid-life values into their theories and reports on old age. A recent theory in the field, called *gerotranscendence*, raises these same questions, and claims that old age has its very own character, meaning, and values quite different from those of mid-life (Tornstam, 2005). Rather than assume that correct or successful aging means to maintain a mid-life pattern of activity well into old age, there is evidence of a continual development of the person into a different mental and behavioral pattern in later life. This different pattern involves a redefinition of the self and relationships to others, as well as a new understanding of basic existential questions concerning life, death, time, and space. The person becomes less self-preoccupied and more selective in the choice of social and other activities. There is less interest in superficial social interaction, and a growing appreciation of solitude as distinct from loneliness. It might well be that earlier findings of loneliness among the elderly are not simply that, but, rather, indicate their preference for more solitude of a contemplative nature. There have been empirical findings to show that much younger age groups report personal feelings of loneliness significantly more than do the eldest age groups. There is also evidence of the development of a cosmic consciousness in later life, or what might be called a sense of greater communion with the spirit of the universe (Atchley, 2009; Hood, 1983; Sherman & Webb, 1994; Tornstam, 2005).

Gerotranscendence claims to be a theory that goes beyond the old dualism of activity versus disengagement. It goes beyond them by uncovering and describing a whole new set of dimensions in the life experience of many elderly. These new dimensions were found through extensive survey research and, particularly, from in-depth interviews with many older persons (Dalby, 2006; Levinson et al., 2005). Most of this research has been done in Scandinavia, so there are inevitable questions about possible value preferences that are different from the largely American conception of successful old age. These are legitimate research concerns, and they became very personal concerns to me as I approached and entered into retirement. I have continued to do scholarly research and writing on these issues during retirement. At the same time, I have also been counseling elders, many of whom have reported experiencing transcendent experiences, as described in the theory of gerotranscendence. These elements are at the heart of contemplative aging, and they will be explored here in depth along with other developments in old age that have been found through reputable gerontological study and research.

Retirement turns out to be an unexpectedly complex process, hardly a quick and definitive act or event. For most of us, retirement means that we can begin to devote more of our time to activities we cherish: recreational, creative, charitable, familial, or any combination of these and others. Indeed, it is that, but it is also a transition into the last stage of life, to becoming "old"—a condition dreaded by many, and a word that is, therefore, often avoided. One editorial in a leading gerontological journal, *The Gerontologist,* advised against use of the term "old," and advised that it should be seen as a form of "ageism" in scientific gerontological language, if not in common language. The editorial even bemoaned the use of "aging" as a code word for deterioration. Instead, terms such as "older person," "retired person," "senior," even "persons older than sixty" were proposed as preferable for scientific writing.

Rather than scientific, much of this seems euphemistic and unnecessary. Actually, the Latin roots of old are *alere*, meaning to nourish, and *alescere* to grow. There is a sense in which these ancient meanings endure, although it is not a literal or obvious one; and it is the exploration and elaboration of this sense to which much of this book is devoted. To me, the word "old" infers "venerable," and I cannot think of a term that implies venerable more clearly than the word "elder." So elder is used herein as much as possible, in preference to such terms as older person, older adult, senior, and so on. Additionally, the word "old" is be used unabashedly throughout the book since, as an octogenarian, I should qualify as old according to anyone's definition of that term. Presumably that might provide me some license to write about the experience of growing old and retiring, without being charged as biased against the old.

From this perspective, I must say that many of the things my colleagues and I have written about later life, based on the "objective" findings of gerontological research and practice, feel different when experienced personally. Some of our quantitative findings need to be qualified from the qualitative perspective of lived experience, as reported by elders in gerotranscendence studies (Lewin & Thomas, 2001; Tornstam, 1997; Wink & Dillon, 2002). Like the majority of my colleagues, I did most of my research and practice in my middle years, but it is another thing to shift from that professional perspective and begin looking at aging from within the actual experience of growing old oneself. Continuing to counsel elders in my retirement keeps me in touch with the inner and outer experiences of their lives. This has convinced me that a contemplative old age is something that can be developed in the natural course of aging, if that is our inclination and our desire. All it needs is recognition and cultivation.

It should be said, however, that there are prevailing societal and cultural attitudes that tend to devalue and, thereby, suppress these natural inclinations. These countervailing attitudes will become apparent in the first chapter, beginning with a personal experience, and then expanded upon in terms of retirement and "aging out" in our society generally. The process of overcoming these societal and cultural constraints calls for a degree of acceptance and practice that allows the natural inclinations to emerge, and enables one to lead to a truly contemplative and rewarding old age. This book will attempt to make the nature of that acceptance and practice explicit and accessible.

What is meant by contemplative aging? Most dictionaries define contemplation as "to view or consider with continued attention," to meditate on, or ponder. In some traditions, it is a religious discipline of prayer and meditation on spiritual matters, but in this book it is meant in a more general sense, which may or may not be religious but can certainly be spiritual. It is a way of aging in the latter stages of life, in which there exists both greater indwelling and considering—"with continued attention"—the meaning and experience of one's own being. In one sense, this is an existential or philosophical kind of attention, not as formal philosophical study, but as viewing one's life *in toto*, from past to present to future, especially "in the moment," so as to understand or comprehend it to the extent possible.

In addition to this philosophical aspect of contemplative aging, there is another aspect that is psychological in nature. Perhaps it is best described in terms of what is called "contemplative psychology," a relatively new field that involves study of the methods and psychological effects of contemplative practices throughout recorded human history, in both Eastern and Western traditions. It has extracted and described those elements which are central to all the traditions. It describes their aim as a way of *being* that includes "a first-person form of knowing that possesses intimacy and directness." It is based on "a . . . *here and now awareness* of one's unveiled experience of reality, and includes a direct, nonconceptual experience of one's own existence" (de Wit, 1991, p. 33). Intuition is central to this kind of knowing, since it bypasses conceptual thinking, memory, and the senses. Actually, the word *intuition* comes from the Latin *intueri*, which means to look toward or *to contemplate*. Contemplative psychologies contain methods of eliciting this kind of knowing through meditation, introspection, prayer, and other contemplative practices directed toward mental clarity, insight, and illumination. The one common characteristic of these methods is that they are indwelling, i.e., going inward so as to remove external distractions as much as possible in order to enhance contemplation. When all is said and done, this amounts to a *praxis*, or set of practices, of a psycho-philosophical nature, which are actually a way of knowing and being, and an approach to reality and enlightenment.

The reader for whom this book might have the most immediate resonance and meaning could well be the more introspective or introverted kind of person. Older introverts have lived their young and middle years in a highly extraverted society, usually attempting to make their social personas over into the appearance of someone they are not. If there is any time they can truly become themselves, it is in old age and retirement. This is not to say that extraverted individuals cannot benefit from a more contemplative old age; indeed, they can. My own gerontological practice and research, and that of others, show that they can, and do, but it does not come as naturally to them as it does to more introspective folk. Both types of individuals have the innate capacity to pursue a rewarding contemplative old age, because it is a natural process, if allowed to emerge and develop. The critical point is to become conscious of it, and then to live it and practice it in full consciousness. It is a natural path and practice, especially in later life, and this book is intended to show how it can be realized.

Those readers who wish to go directly into the practice methods of this contemplative way of being can begin with Chapter Five. The philosophical and psychological foundations, as well as the gerontological research evidence, covered in the first four chapters, can be read before, after, or concurrently with the actual contemplative practice. What matters is beginning and staying with the practice and the wisdom that form the essence of this way of being in late life.

Chapter One

From Doing to Being

There is a gradual but observable shift in the balance of activity to rest or repose as we move into the later years of life. Most of the time the inevitable physical limitations of advancing age dictate the need to be less active, but where there are no such limitations, there is still an implicit need to find one's own mix of activity and repose. At another level, this can be viewed as the ontological balance or mix of doing to being. Even at this level, there seems to be a cultural imperative to remain as active as possible well into very old age, so we have the feeling that we *have* to choose the *vita activa* over the *vita contemplativa* until we are quite old and decrepit. Formal retirement is frequently the occasion on which the meaning of this becomes radically apparent and needs to be confronted, publicly and privately, as occurred in my own retirement experience, which follows.

The Bearable Lightness of Being . . . Retired

My apologies to Milan Kundera (1984) for this play on the title of his novel, *The Unbearable Lightness of Being*, but it captures a perplexing aspect of aging that begins with retirement. The idea that retirement could be at all puzzling came as a personal surprise. After all, it was something I had planned for, both financially and psychologically, for many years. Yet even before the formal date of my retirement, I came to realize that it presents a dilemma having to do with lightness and weightiness in Kundera's sense of these terms.

This became apparent in the question I was asked repeatedly by friends and colleagues, "What are you going to *do* in your retirement?" My usual response was to tell them of my plans for travel and relaxation. This would elicit smiles of approval and the usual statements of envy, but it quickly became apparent that this was only about the "light" side of retirement. Beneath this amiable kind of discourse on the subject was the heavier question of "What are you going to do in retirement, *seriously*?" I soon realized that I would have to come up with an explanation of what I would be "doing" in retirement that would be considered "meaningful" or useful. So, in answer to that, I would reply that I was going to continue my counseling practice with elders, and to write a book about the lives and aging experiences of certain exceptional older persons whom I had interviewed in the course of field research on the subject of reminiscence in later life. My hope was that they could serve as exemplars for older persons in the general reading public. That sounded both serious and useful, so it satisfied my interlocutors. Still, I was beginning to be troubled about being asked the same question, with its inherent weightiness, "What are you going to *do* in retirement?" I was developing a nagging impulse to respond, "How about *being*? What would it be like to just *be* rather than *do*?"

Actually, I did respond in that way to one colleague, and he was nonplused. He gave me an uncertain look, wondering if I was pulling his leg; then he laughed rather tentatively and, sure enough, he said, "No, I mean, what are you going to do, *seriously*?" By this time the whole subject had turned itself back on me, and I had to ask myself, "But, seriously, what about *being*? What is it? It can't just mean taking it easy." I needed to think about it more carefully and deeply. I knew, of course, that being and doing cannot be separated in any realistic sense; that would be illusory. There is always a shifting but inseparable mix of one as related to the other. After all, just sitting with an empty mind is *doing* something. However, I couldn't help but think that, after almost a half century of *doing* and teaching in the human services and sciences, there had to be some shift along the continuum toward being, whatever that might be. Most certainly I felt a strong inner pull in that direction.

What did Kundera have to say about this? What did he mean by the "lightness" of being? As I reread his novel, he seemed to be putting the question in the context of our "doings" in the world, our actions and involvements with the people and things of the world. He seemed particularly taken by our existential responsibility for these actions and involvements. He regarded this responsibility as heavy, a burden, and stated, "The heavier the burden, the closer our lives come to earth, the more real and truthful they become. Conversely, the absolute absence of a burden causes man to be lighter than air, to soar into the heights, take leave of the earth and his earthly being, and become only half real, his movements as free as they are insignificant." (Kundera, 1984, p. 5).

So, in its utter lightness, being lacks significance. That seemed "heavy" in the vernacular sense, and hard to take in the conceptual sense.

Certainly there was something missing in his assessment of being. Actually, he admitted that the ancient Greek sage and philosopher Parmenides held that lightness is positive and weight negative. This led him to ask whether Parmenides was correct or not. After mulling it over, all he could come up with was the statement that "the only certainty is: the lightness/weight opposition is the most mysterious, most ambiguous of all." He might have been mystified by this, but I was even more perplexed about his notion that the lightness of being is insignificant and, therefore, unbearable, particularly with respect to what I was undergoing in my own retirement experience. One way to remove some of the ambiguity is to take a look at what it means to be in retirement within the real context of our current American society.

Doing and Being in Retirement

Erik Erikson (1968), in his influential study of the human life cycle, *Childhood and Society*, found that the mature personality expresses itself in both action and contemplation; and he raised the question of whether a culture that almost exclusively emphasizes action can be a very healthy environment for human growth. This question obviously has meaning for growing old as well as for growing up in such a culture. Now Erikson posed the issue in terms of action and contemplation, but it has to be put in the larger framework of doing and being. If one is contemplating, isn't one *doing* something? It would seem so, even if only in the semantic sense. Nevertheless, there can and should be a difference in emphasis, in time and attention devoted to each, under different circumstances and in different stages of our lives. The argument being made here is that later life, from roughly age sixty on, is the prime time to be more contemplative. If not in old age, when?

"What do you *do?*" is the central existential question in a society devoted to the production and consumption of goods and services. Elders who are no longer "meaningfully" employed in production or consumption find themselves lacking any clear sense of social identity. The question then becomes, as I was asked so frequently by friends and family, "What *will* you do when you retire?" One option is to become more of a consumer of travel, recreation, and entertainment services and commodities, but the underlying question is, then, whether this is meaningful in any sense beyond the mere doing. Volunteering is an alternative to the consumer role, and it is becoming very popular and widespread among elders. It is a form of doing that can provide some sense of meaning in retirement, and is increasingly being pursued with that in mind. Yet one wonders how often it is being pursued because of the unbearable lightness of simply being. As e. e. cummings once put it, "If you can be, be. If not, cheer up and go on about other people's business, doing and undoing to others 'til you drop."

How can retirement—a word that evokes images of relaxation and recreation—be considered not only perplexing but also traumatic? Some leading gerontologists have claimed that, indeed, it can be traumatic, because so much of our sense of self-worth and identity has been defined by what we do, by our occupations and our performance in productive social roles. From that perspective, retirement and its implications of non-doing can threaten us to the core. It can amount to what Erikson would call a major psycho-social crisis in life, much like the oft-cited mid-life crisis. Currently, there continues to be an emphasis on doing in our culture, still with the imperative to "stay active," but in different ways. Euphemistic terms such as "redeployment" or "redirection" have been used by gerontologists to describe this shift. Thus, "productive" retirement involves keeping busy with volunteer activities, attending educational, health, and cultural programs and events, and other socially approved and valued activities. These activities have unquestionable social and survival value, but there is a marketing flavor to much of this approach, as can be seen in AARP publications and products. Something is lacking in this scenario, namely the more interior and reflective features of mental life that emerge during the later years, which are much more about being than doing. When one considers retirement in the original meaning of the term, it is to "pull back," to "take stock," to review and consider the whole. However, the current popular *and* professional view of "successful" aging does not seem to allow much room for these being needs of late life, which are needs of a more interior and contemplative nature.

One eminent gerontologist wrote an editorial entitled "The Myth of Successful Aging" (Cohler, 1992), in which the contemporary discussions of aging assume the continued importance of individual activity and achievement of early and middle adult life into old age, without this interior or spiritual dimension. He claimed the emphasis is "scientistic" in stressing maintenance of health with a view to the realization of successful aging. These high expectations of continued achievement, robust health, and personal well-being have led to a situation, especially among professional men and women, in which retirement is most often viewed as anathema. For them, "being" in retirement *would* have an unbearable lightness.

This was not always the case with professionals entering retirement. William James, whose rich melding of psychology and philosophy still has so much to contribute to our modern understanding of the aging process, was one such professional. When he retired from the philosophy department at Harvard, in January 1907, he said that, henceforth, he would be free to live "for truth pure and simple, instead of for truth accommodated to the most unheard of requirements set by others." There is no question that he had taken a distinctly contemplative turn by the time of his retirement. More remarkable was the exemplary man of action, George Washington, who on his retirement from command of the victorious Continental Army, wrote the following to the Marquis de Lafayette: "I am not only retired from all public employments but I am retiring within myself, and shall be able to view the solitary walk and tread the paths of private life with heartfelt satisfaction. Envious of none, I am determined to be pleased with all; and this, my dear friend, being the order of my march, I will move gently down the stream of life until I sleep with my fathers" (Randall, 1998). More recently, a newly retired professor of English wrote in a gerontological journal that she was heartened by the fact that writers such as May Sarton, Doris Grumbach, and Doris Lessing use time differently in their older years, by immersing and rejuvenating themselves in nature and thus transcending quotidian time. She hailed the fact that they rejected "the popular notion of 'productive' aging, such as keeping busy with volunteer activities, playing golf, interacting with younger folks, traveling, and attending cultural events. For those writers aging becomes not a social and physical phenomenon, but a metaphysical one" (Waxman, 1999, p. 516).

On a folksier note, a fellow retiree drafted a letter to the editor of a local newspaper about a recent article in the business section, written by a Mr. Harvey, which "extolled the virtues of non-retirement." The letter writer sardonically disagreed, saying that as a recent retiree he wanted to "be among the first to slap old Harvey on the back and applaud his can-do spirit." He continued, tongue-in-cheek, saying "It is only the heroic and self denying sacrifice of those who persist in spinning the laboratory cartwheel that permits the escapees to roam free," and he encouraged Harvey to "keep up the good work."

Here, surely, is testimony to the bearable lightness of *retirement*, and, perhaps, of simply *being*. One dictionary definition of the word retirement is "retreat, withdrawal for prayer, study, or meditation," and in cultures of the past and present, arrangements for such retreats or withdrawals have been built into the social fabric of each culture. This has been true of Christian as well as Hindu and Buddhist cultures, and it continues to be available in other contemporary societies. A psychologist and expert in cross-cultural studies of aging, David Gutmann (1974), described his experience with this phenomenon, in a study of Druze elders living in Israel. Most Druze live in neighboring Lebanon and Syria, and they are village-dwelling herdsmen and farmers of the Galilean highlands. They are considered heretics in Islam by other Muslims, but they have maintained their cultural heritage and continuity in that region for over 800 years, in the face of much persecution. Consequently, some of the core features of individual Druze character are stubbornness, piety, and reserve. Older men are held in high regard, and Druze patriarchs have a great deal of political, economic, and religious power. During the first stage of his study, Gutmann, interviewed a Druze elder in his early seventies who was an influential and respected leader in his community. The villagers would come to this man for advice and decisions on family, property, and ethical dilemmas. He would have to mediate family conflicts and neighbor squabbles over issues such as how many goats were a fair trade for a piece of land, or a charge that someone stole someone else's goat. He confided in Gutmann that he was growing weary of these responsibilities, and found them to be an increasing burden. He said he would very much like to retire from them, but he felt compelled by his stature in the community to carry on.

That interview marked the "before" part of Gutmann's longitudinal study of older men. When he returned five years later to interview this same elder, for the "after" part of the study, he knocked at the front door of the man's house, and the man's wife appeared at the door. When he asked to talk to her husband, she answered with a trace of peevishness, "He's where he spends almost all of his time lately, out in back in the prayer house." Gutmann proceeded out to the rear of the man's property and found him in the small, single-room structure, engrossed in prayer or meditation. The elder recognized him immediately, and with a benign smile on his face, told him that several months earlier he finally did what he wanted, i.e., to retire from those patriarchal duties. He went on to say that he had never felt such peace and contentment in his life.

Gutmann and his colleagues, in the field of study called the psychology of aging, refer to this man's transformation as a move from "autoplastic mastery" to "omniplastic mastery." They have found the same phenomenon among men of the remote, preliterate Highland Maya of Mexico, and it was originally found among American men (Gutmann, 1964). Based on their studies of men, there appear to be three stages that men go through. In the first one, termed *alloplastic* mastery, which begins in the twenties and runs into the early fifties, the emphasis is on pursuit of achievement and independence, as well as on control of outer world affairs. The second stage, which occurs in the fifties and sixties, is termed *autoplastic* mastery, and the emphasis is on more accommodation to the outer world, and on changing one's self rather than the external environment. Gutmann and his colleagues called this "passive mastery," because thought begins to replace action more and more often. From the seventies on, men move into the last stage, which the researchers termed *omniplastic* or "magical" mastery, characterized by greater engagement in recollection and reverie rather than in instrumental action, either in the outer world or within the self. They also said it was marked by "philosophic resignation," because they tended to see these late changes as defensive and regressive. This could well be a value judgment on the part of Gutmann and his colleagues, who were in the alloplastic stage of life themselves.

Overall, then, what we see is a change in the way people conduct and see themselves in relationship to their surroundings and circumstances. Whereas in their younger years they are apt to try to actively or aggressively remake or reshape their physical and social environments, in the later years they attempt to handle or adapt to each new circumstance in a more reflective and accommodating way, so as to minimize stress and conserve energy. Part of this modality is a protective or defensive measure, to feel more secure in what, perhaps, appears as a more complex or threatening world to them. However, this can also be seen as a move toward greater acceptance and valuing of what one already has. Gutmann has described this as a turn away from competition and achievement toward the more elemental and sacred aspects of life. This was certainly so in the case of the Druze elder he interviewed, in whom inner, more passive and more imaginative forms of mastery, such as prayer, meditation, and recollection, replaced many of the external forms of mastery. Rather than being seen as regressive, these changes can be seen as stages of development to be realized and maximized in their own right. They can also be seen as another instance of a shift from a doing toward a being orientation toward life. It needs to be said, again, that doing and being are inseparable and innate polarities of our existence. They cannot be separated experientially, only abstractly, in a discursive context such as this. Contemplation, as we have said, is *doing* something. However, this particular kind of doing requires some change in attitude and habitual patterns of living, to allow for its emergence and practice in everyday life. The capacity for making this move occurs rather naturally in the course of aging but, again, it has to be recognized and cultivated for it to be realized in later life.

There is something about the view from old age that even insightful, younger persons can intuit as somehow more elevated or encompassing than their own youthful perspective. Rainer Maria Rilke intuited this in his younger years when he wrote, "I believe in old age; to work and to grow old: this is what life expects of us. And then one day *to be old* and still be quite far from understanding everything—no, but to begin, to love, but to suspect, but to be connected to what is remote and inexpressible, all the way up to the stars" (2006, p. 25). This certainly appears to be an intuition of cosmic consciousness in old age from a younger vantage point.

The Interiority of Late Life

This ontological shift has been found by research psychologists in the field of aging to be a natural development in later life, and it has been described as an increased "interiority" of the personality. It is a development that tends to occur around the time people are entering their sixties (Neugarten, 1973). The research findings show that middle-aged Americans, in their forties and fifties, tend to see themselves as having enough energy and "go-getiveness" to overcome obstacles and take advantage of opportunities in the environment, whereas those sixty and over tend to see themselves as accommodating more to the outer world. The researchers have described this as a shift from an active to a passive form of mastery, as individuals move from middle into old age. The word "passive" has a pejorative connotation in our society, but here it means that the use of mental capacities, like memory and imagination, become more prominent in later life relative to motility and action in dealing with the environment, with one's own body, and with life's circumstances. This form of mastery is marked by an increasing commitment to a central core of values and ways of behaving and relating to the outside world. At the same time, with this turn inward, many of the old attachments and animosities, likes and dislikes, alliances, grudges, and ambitions lose their hold on people. Elders feel more able to concentrate on their core values, on the cohesion and continuity of the essential elements of their personalities, and on the meaning of their lives.

As you might imagine, this kind of transformation is much less obvious in America than in other places, where the culture recognizes and supports this kind of development in later life. Yet it does happen to Americans, as the research shows, and this interiority allows for emerging inner capacities that can compensate for, and even transcend, the physical and social losses of later life. On this view, youth would be defined as the period requiring the gathering and enlarging of strength and experience, whereas later life would be defined as the period of clarifying and deepening what has already been attained and learned from experience and adaptation across the life span. Thus, it has been proposed that the inward-turning process of interiority can represent a key developmental gain in facilitating the kind of integration, or "ego integrity," that Erik Erikson sees as desirable in late life. Similarly, Carl Jung's individuation process of balance and wholeness in maturity has been viewed as a kind of socialization to this introversion, "an education of the soul," to complement the extraverted style of our formal schooling and culture at large (Storr, 1983).

We can shift from predominant doing to greater being for perhaps the first time in our lives. At any rate, it is all very natural in that we age, that our bodies age, and that we can't extend ourselves outside ourselves as much to change our environments as we were able to do in the past. So it becomes more natural to go within ourselves. Even if this is viewed as simply an accommodation to the physical frailties and social losses of old age, this developing interiority follows a path that has been pursued by monks and mystics for centuries. It is a simplification of the outer life and the enrichment of an inner life. In a sense, all elders follow this path, whether they like it or not. However, the kind of inner life they develop is crucial. If it is filled with regrets for what is missing from their outer lives, despair is the likely outcome. Elders would do well to note what Montaigne had to say about interiority: "It is an absolute perfection and virtually divine to know how to enjoy our being rightfully. We seek other conditions because we do not understand the use of our own and go outside ourselves because we do not know what it is like inside" (Montaigne, 1952, p. 543). This is a sage observation for later life.

Contemplative Being

Milan Kundera's metaphor on the unbearable lightness of being can be viewed much differently from the perspective of old age. He was not, after all, an old man when he wrote the book. There is not only a development toward interiority and more passivity in old age, but there is an existential and experiential shift of foreground and background, in terms of letting heaviness down and allowing lightness to arise. Perhaps it is the passivity of letting the weight fall that makes the lightness of being "unbearable" for Kundera. Before retirement we are always "on the make," striving to achieve something so as to feel good or worthwhile, as well as secure. Letting go after retirement means letting the heaviness down, but we do not feel entitled to letting the burden down.

The shift is toward allowing and acceptance, but we fight it because we feel that we have to struggle and "fight the good fight," which gives us the feeling of strength, mass, and substance. We feel *insubstantial* if we are not making matters weighty. This mind set has a great deal to do with the place of work in contemporary society. We are all, whether professional or nonprofessional workers, functionaries in a social system marked by a division of labor, whereby each of us is allotted a place and function within the system. We might have voluntarily planned and prepared for this function through training and education, but once we are in it, we are functionaries in a world of "total work." It is total in the sense that it determines the conditions and circumstances not only of our actual work activities but also of our leisure. True leisure as a cultural phenomenon should not be the inevitable result of a holiday, a weekend, or a vacation of several weeks or longer. From a cultural standpoint, it is really more of an attitude of mind (Pieper, 1963). In contrast to the idea of work as activity, it is an attitude of non-activity, of inward calm and quiescence. It means letting things happen rather than keeping busy as an article of belief.

The quiescence of leisure is a form of silence, which allows for a finer apprehension of the reality around and within us. It has been said that only the silent hear, and those who do not remain silent do not hear. Leisure, then, is a receptive and, therefore, contemplative attitude of mind that is not only the occasion but also the capacity for immersing oneself in a total sense of being in the moment, in the here-and-now, and in the whole of creation. So leisure is the attitude of mind of those who are open to whatever might emerge in their consciousness, and not of those who feel the need to reach and grasp for whatever they think has to be possessed or accomplished.

True leisure is not just a break in one's work for an hour, a day, or even weeks, since those are pauses made for the sake of work, in the sense of refreshing oneself for more work in the near future. Leisure and contemplation are of a different order, outside the closed circle of work-relaxation-work; and they allow us to realize the natural bent of the human mind and spirit, to contemplate the larger whole. If ever there is a time for true leisure it is in retirement. Will we allow ourselves the opportunity to really engage in it? An 81-year-old woman gave this explanation in a survey interview, as part of a larger research project:

> I always had to be accomplishing something. I'm talking about every minute of every day, sunup to sundown. That's how I was brought up. There were no idle hands in our house. Raising my family, a day was wasted unless I sewed a dress and put up a week's worth of soup and darned a dozen socks. Then I did all this all over again, helping my daughter raise her family. Now I'm an old lady and my hands are knotted up with arthritis. There's hardly anything I can work on anymore. I used to wander around the house, muttering, "useless hands, useless life." I certainly couldn't sit on a couch and say it was a good day. Lately, I've decided to stop fighting it. I've been letting

> my mind roam while my hands rest. You know what I'm thinking now? There's not a thing wrong with sitting still. You just have to relax into it.

Emerson (1870, p. 278) put the matter a bit more elegantly when he wrote about the interiority of old age in the following words:

> But the inner life sits at home, and does not learn to do things, nor value these feats at all. 'Tis a quiet, wise perception. It lives in the great present; it makes the present great. This tranquil, well-founded, wide-seeing soul is no express-rider, no attorney, no magistrate: it lies in the sun, and broods on the world. A person of this temper once said to a man of much activity, 'I will pardon you that you do so much, and you me that I do nothing.'

And Euripides says that "Zeus hates busybodies and those who do too much."

It is fair to say that the greatest spiritual task of aging is to shift direction from the mode of doing to the mode of being. Many elders find their lives meaningless because they have derived their meaning completely from the kinds of activities that they are no longer physically capable of doing, such as earning a living, caring for children, serving the community, or even attending religious services that once gave them a sense of meaning. Thus, they feel they have been "reduced" to the state of being. But the reality is that in our younger years, almost all of our doing is to some end, to make a living, to raise children, and so on. We do not cease doing in old age, even very old age, but it is no longer for those pragmatic ends. There is simply no way to be without some kind of doing, even in silent, effortless daydreaming, which is "doing" something, if we recognize, again, that being and doing are inseparable polarities of our lives. Still, when we meditate or dwell in repose, there is a great deal more in that moment of existence. Yet even the nature of doing can take on a new meaning in later life. This happens when we begin to make doing an end in itself rather than a means to an end. This can be a spiritual as well as pleasurable practice. Doing something in the spirit of non-achievement (in itself, for itself) has a good quality to it. You could even say it is an *enlightened* way of doing. Thus, we can engage in the mundane activities of each day mindfully, as though they are rites or acts of reverence in a state of being that truly gives meaning to what has been called "the holiness of everyday life." This can be like entering a new dimension of living, in which you recognize and revere the simple sanctity of being, a dimension you have, perhaps, overlooked, by-passed, or discounted as meaningless in your earlier years of life. Contemplative being, then, is not defined by specific acts of contemplation, but rather by a whole way of existence.

The concept of being has varied in its meaning in different eras. The Hellenic concept of being was the underlying, essential being, the being which is immovable and unchanging. However, in the later Christian era, there arose a conception of being that viewed it as a progression from lower to higher levels of existence. At the lowest level of minerals or inanimate matter there is pure passivity. A stone is totally passive and dependent on outside forces for movement. The next level, plant, is not totally passive, but it has very limited capacity for adaptation to changing circumstances. At the animal level, consciousness appears, and there is a marked shift from passivity to activity, with an emphasis on purposive movement. Finally, at the fourth and human level, there is an "I," or a person with self-consciousness, which marks a greater shift from passivity to activity. With this self-consciousness, there is always the possibility of rising above circumstances, no matter how weighed down by them the person might be. Consequently, the four levels of being were seen as pointing to the ultimate existence—a level of Being *above* the human.

The word "above" suggests reaching and a striving toward the highest, which is ultimate Being, or God. Contrary to this metaphorical upward reach toward the heavens, it is possible to take a different route, which is inward and downward. It is one of letting go and *allowing*, that is, allowing the "gravity" of being, of existence, to predominate, and to move one toward a deeper level of being. This is a conception closer to the Greek. Recall that gravity means not only the gravitational attraction of mass, but it also denotes importance and seriousness. Thus, letting go of the weight of societal roles, responsibilities, and burdens in this metaphor does not make for an "unbearable" lightness of being in the sense of being useless or meaningless.

A most felicitous term in this regard is Paul Tillich's expression "Ground of Being" (1973), which provides a more earthly sense of being in later life. It includes not only the physical and sensuous realm of being, but even the mental realm, which takes on a different tone in late life, one of receptivity and spirituality. Aristotle reminds us that the goal of action is always contemplation, which is knowing and being rather than seeking and becoming. Reflecting and musing, instead of intense searching and examination, becomes the more open and contemplative process of what Heraclitus called "listening to the essence of things." Thoreau put it differently when he wrote, "Wisdom does not inspect, but beholds." Therein lies the holiness of contemplative being in later life. It is becoming one with Being.

Chapter Two

Philosophical Aging

In his influential paradigm of the stages of human development, Erik Erikson (1982) claimed that the last developmental task of life is to find an assured sense of meaning and order in one's life and in the universe. The way for elders to achieve that assured sense is to develop a particular style of old age, which he called "philo-sophical," inserting a hyphen to emphasize the original Greek meaning, *philo* (love) and *sophia* (wisdom), or love of wisdom. Such a love enables one to maintain order and meaning in the disintegration of mind and body, while also advocating a "durable hope in wisdom" (Erikson, 1982, p. 64). By this philosophical attitude Erikson meant not only a calm and unflinching attitude in the face of trouble, pain, and loss, but also an open and reflective frame of mind, which allows one to ponder the place and meaning of that pain, and those losses, in the context of both one's entire life and place in the universe.

Erikson was referring to a psychological development that ordinarily occurs in old age in the normal course of aging. But what if one goes directly to philosophy itself to further develop this frame of mind as a way of life in old age? Although much of philosophy deals in abstractions, there is a wealth of wisdom to be unearthed in reading some of its greatest practitioners, especially those who saw philosophy as a way of life (Hadot, 1995). It can certainly strengthen and add substance to the philosophical style that Erikson claimed emerges in later life, as a natural development of aging.

The Consolations of Philosophy

One of the most powerful examples of philosophy as a way of life was given by Boethius (1962), in his classic book *The Consolation of Philosophy*. This learned and accomplished man was unjustly accused of treason and sacrilege in 523 CE, and thrown into a remote prison of the Roman Empire, where he suffered deprivation and torture for months before his brutal execution. Yet in those trying months, he wrote *The Consolation* in his prison cell, and it became one of the most influential books in Western Europe from the late Middle Ages until the end of the

Renaissance. It was remarkable for its curative power as a remedy against desolation of the spirit in the face of much misfortune, pain, material deprivation, and injustice in the course of life. For Boethius, philosophy truly was the love of wisdom, in terms of its liberating power of mind, and in providing a true estimate of the limited value of transitory material and physical satisfactions in life. Furthermore, he rendered this attitude beautifully in the poetic form of that period.

Although Boethius was a devout Christian, he consoled himself through philosophy alone, not Christian doctrine. Of course, it is entirely possible that philosophy for him was influenced by his strong religious beliefs. In fact, he did claim that philosophy teaches us that the supreme good and highest happiness are found in God and, in fact, *are* God. This raises a question as to whether there were other precedents in Western philosophy for a contemplative way of life that were not bound to the prevailing conception of God found in Christianity or the other major monotheistic religions. Where might a modern secular person look for a philosophy, rather than a theology, with sufficient mental and emotional sustenance to provide a truly contemplative way of life in old age? The ancient philosophy of Plotinus is one that could conceivably qualify, and Plotinus lived and taught in Rome even before Boethius, circa 205-270 CE. For him, philosophy was a route to what today might be called a conversion, meaning a return to the self, to its essence. He believed that, in our ordinary state of consciousness, we are spiritually distant and distracted from the true self, and this calls for a major reorientation of our attention inward. The philosophical life is a constant quest, seeking to find the prior unity of the Good or the One, which is the ground or ultimate source of spiritual life. The One is pure, simple, and indecomposable presence. This quest is an experiential one that goes beyond normal reason and intellect, transcending our ordinary discursive consciousness. Through contemplation, the soul can reach its highest state, which is one of receptive passivity. He wrote, "The soul's highest state is complete passivity," and he invites us to bring about this form of passivity in ourselves (Hadot, 1993, p.8). It is in such a state that one is apt to have contact with the "Good" (*qua* God), in a mystical experience of union. This is not that far removed spiritually from Boethius. Such an experience of union cannot be willed, so we cannot know with certainty if it will come about. Yet one continues preparing for it through contemplation, which nevertheless has its own rewards in its very practice.

The central doctrine in Plotinus's philosophy has to do with three realities of ascending value and unity. They are Soul, Mind (*Nous*), and the highest first principle, which Plotinus, like Plato, called the One or the Good. Thus, rather than the monotheistic God, there is the One or the Good, and through contemplation the individual can approach the One through the levels or realities of Soul and Mind. This contemplative practice calls for a turn inward toward the self, not to seek refuge or satisfaction within one's self, but because, through its conversion to interiority, the human self transcends itself and no longer sees itself as an isolated ego. At this level of transformation, there is an experience of an other than self, i.e., it is an experience of oneself becoming Other, of unity with the One. This is not unlike the Hindu view of self as related to, and absorbed in, the larger universal Self or Atman.

Plotinus proposed that what matters in the contemplative life is that we rid ourselves of "having" in order "to be," in its purest sense. This means simplicity in worldly possessions, thought, and deed. True being is the first level of reality that proceeds from the One, for actually the One is beyond being, and the source of being. Being is the ultimate simplicity of life, and it is incapable of being grasped by reflection. In order to reach it and our pure self, we have to abandon intellectual reflection for contemplation; but even then, we can only identify ourselves with our true self for a few fleeting moments. At our ordinary level of consciousness and ego self, all we can access are fleeting thoughts and images. We attempt to fixate the content of this stream in language, but it just brings us back to the intellect and reason, which cannot reach the realm of clear and simple being. Yet for Plotinus, the spiritual realm was nothing other than the self at its deepest level, and it can be reached by returning within oneself at any time. This is achieved without ritual and without the theological superstructure of institutionalized religion. Yet who can say that these returns within the self that Plotinus describes are not genuinely spiritual, if not religious, experiences?

There is no question where Plotinus stood with respect to the issue of contemplation versus action. He claimed that when people are too weak for contemplation they switch to action, which he described as but a mere shadow of contemplation and reason. Contemplation was at the center of his ontology. For him, experiential life consisted of contemplation, concrete simplicity, and presence. In this respect, his approach was very similar to some forms of Eastern meditation and mindfulness, of being present in the now, and apprehending life's grace directly—experientially rather than intellectually. He valued intuition over intellect in the life of reason, and through this he grasped the ultimate foundation of life as grace. He claimed "The Good is gentle, mild, and very delicate, and always at the disposition of whomever desires it" (Hadot, 1993, p.60). This statement could serve as an apt description of Plotinus himself, a person who displayed gentleness, a tactful sense of reality, and a smiling benevolence, despite a very distressing physical affliction he endured in his later years of life. Not a bad model for the philosophical style of old age proposed by Erikson!

The alternative to adopting this style of old age, Erikson (1982) claimed, is dogmatism, and a "compulsive pseudointegrity" that can become a "coercive orthodoxy." This is usually expressed in rigid attitudes and beliefs about how one's life should be lived and understood, generally through highly conventional and orthodox social and religious views instilled in us in childhood, and accepted and reinforced throughout the life cycle into old age. If unquestioning acceptance of the received wisdom of their respective religions accounts for this failure to address the issue of life's meaning, then one would have to agree with theologian Paul Tillich (1955), when he noted that many believers end up in a state of spiritual infancy, "the state of being a babe in thinking, unable to receive solid food, milk-fed only." Emerson went further, when he stated that the faith that stands on authority is no faith at all; it is dogmatic belief, perhaps, but not faith. So what is to follow is not for the person whose faith stands on authority, the "true believer," but one who is open to a broader and, perhaps, more philosophical approach to meaning and faith in later life.

A Philosophical Way

What the philosophical style calls for in old age is an openness of mind that is both seeking of and receptive to ways of being and becoming, which are not necessarily prescribed or preordained by any particular familial, social, religious, or other belief system. Karl Jaspers (1967), the twentieth century German philosopher, proposed a philosophical way of life commensurable with Erikson's philosophical style. He called it "philosophical faith," which is a faith that relies on reason and intuition rather than revelation, prophetic beliefs, or doctrine. Yet he realized that reason, by itself, is not adequate to the task. He envisioned a faith that goes beyond our empirical existence and strives toward being, which is "beyond the world to the ground of existence in the world." Reason can only take us up to the horizon of life in this world, to the point of transcendence and metaphysics, but then in our seeking we have to rely on the "ciphers" that intimate what is "beyond." Ciphers are found in the symbolic forms of insight we gain through art, poetry, mythology, religion and nature itself, but they can only point us toward rather than take us to what Paul Tillich called the Ground of Being. Jaspers claimed that our only access to "the incomprehensible, the inconceivable, the all-encompassing, is by the ever-inadequate, endlessly variable ciphers." This calls for a kind of faith, since there is no sure way to ultimate truth or reality, only the seeking and intuiting through ciphers and reason. William James (1956) had earlier written of the human need for a philosophical faith of this sort, when he commented on the inner need of believing that this world of nature is a sign of something more spiritual and eternal than its material existence.

Philosophy as a way of life for Jaspers was identified with philosophic thinking itself, contemplation rather than any particular set of hypotheses, syllogisms, or conclusions. His philosophy was an effort to explore the margins and limits of our empirical existence, the indefinite horizon in which the distinction between subject and object can be transcended. He used the term *das Umgreifende*, "the encompassing," to refer to the ultimate range of being. We will have occasion to come back to this concept of the *encompassing*, for it can carry us beyond the limits of Jaspers' own existentialist philosophy to a way of being that is more inclusive and applicable for a fully contemplative later life. Jaspers recognized that existentialist philosophy is largely tied to reason, and is incapable of knowing the limits of being. It can only capture fragmentary representations of it in ciphers, which is a limitation that requires philosophical faith. Intellectual reason can only point vaguely and reach gropingly toward aspects of a reality beyond the empirically known limits of being, toward Kant's *Ding-an-sich* or "thing-in-itself." Thus, it lacks the means to provide the transcendent view or spiritual sustenance one might seek in later life, when facing one's finitude. According to Jaspers, it is only if there is a larger, more encompassing, consciousness beyond our cognitive minds available to us that we can know and enter into the ultimate reality of being. This means a consciousness that goes beyond our conventional dualistic views of what is real or unreal and right or wrong in any ultimate sense. Intellectual speculation, logical reasoning, or setting moral imperatives will not do it. What we need is a way to approach it and intuit something of it through a contemplative practice and way of being. The philosophical attitude or style that Erikson and Jaspers refer to is certainly a beginning.

The Psychological Dimension

Although my personal conclusion in Chapter One was that the lightness of being *is* bearable, that still leaves open the question of just what being *is*. Indeed, much of twentieth century philosophy was deeply concerned with this question. Heidegger, in his monumental *Being and Time*, began with a question that haunted him for the rest of his life: "Do we in our time have an answer to the question of what we really mean by the word 'being'? Not at all. So it is fitting that we should raise anew the question of the meaning of Being" (1962, p. 1). He then began a detailed study of the contents of daily existence, using a "hermeneutic phenomenological" method of dense complexity. This was published as *Being and Time* in 1927, but at the end he had to admit that the question of being was still a dark and mysterious one. Later in the century, Jean Paul Sartre (1966), in *Being and Nothingness*, also probed the complex dimensions of this immense area of philosophy known as ontology, or the study of the nature of being. Yet, the question of being versus doing that was raised in Chapter One does not have to entail an abstract ontological analysis. We can ask what being is like as we experience it, feel it, and think about it. That question takes us into the psychological dimension of being as well as the philosophical, and it calls for a combined psycho-philosophical exploration. As noted earlier, a number of findings from research on the psychology of aging indicate some developments toward a more contemplative way of being in old age. The findings of increased interiority of the personality and of elders engaging in a life review process are among those developments. In pursuing the implications of these psychological developments as a gerontologist, I have found that the writers and thinkers who were most helpful in the study of this dimension were either psychologists or psychiatrists with a strong philosophical interest and knowledge base and philosophers with a strong psychological orientation and foundation. Erikson himself is representative of this orientation, in that he was a psychiatrist who obviously saw the philosophical as well as the psychological and social dimensions of human development throughout the life cycle. Karl Jaspers, whose writings on philosophical faith and the *encompassing* have already been mentioned, was a research psychiatrist who developed a rigorous, scientifically-based description of psychopathology in his *General Psychopathology* in 1913. However, his first love became philosophy, which he taught at the University of Heidelberg, from 1921 until 1937, and then, later, at the University of Basel in Switzerland, where he published his three volume magnum opus *Philosophy* (1932).

William James had a career trajectory very similar to Jaspers'. He also studied medicine, and his interest turned to research psychology at Harvard, where he wrote his immensely influential *Principles of Psychology,* published in 1890. Yet he, too, turned to philosophy, which he taught at Harvard until his retirement almost two decades later. A number of his psychological and philosophical insights are central to this exploration of contemplative aging. Parenthetically, even Sartre (1948) turned to psychology in his phenomenological study of human imagination. Other psychological thinkers and psychologists are drawn upon in the course of this book, but the basic psychological evidence for a contemplative later life comes primarily from the empirical findings of gerontological research and practice.

Contemplative psychology is a relatively new field concerned with researching and describing the methods and spiritual disciplines, past and present, that humans have used in living a more contemplative existence. A number of spiritual traditions, both Western and Eastern, have implicit psychologies that provide explicit methods and practices for living such an existence. Two of the contributors to this relatively new field are Han de Wit (1991), a Dutch psychologist who wrote *Contemplative Psychology*, and Gerald May (1982), an American psychiatrist who wrote *Will and Spirit: A Contemplative Psychology.* According to their view, the aim of contemplative psychology is to study and describe a way of being that incorporates a way of *knowing* free from confusion about the *ap-*

pearance of things, as opposed to what they really are. This kind of knowing should provide an increased capacity to remain open to what is called the *basic ground of reality*, in its most pristine aspects and features. This involves sharpening one's mindfulness, awareness, and intuition through contemplative practices. These capacities can only be experienced in the first person mode, in our own individual mental domains. Academic psychology has, for the most part, rejected introspection or other attempts to observe one's own mind in favor of an "objective" or outside observer frame of reference. Contemplative psychology, on the other hand, considers the mental domain to be an observable and legitimate realm of study; thus, it views any methodology that limits the object of investigation to what can be explored only in the third-person mode as fundamentally incomplete. The approach taken here is much the same as William James' "radical empiricism," by which he was able to study and describe, both introspectively and objectively, mental phenomena with enduring effectiveness and lucidity.

We humans are conditioned from infancy on about the way things are by our parents, family, society, and culture in general. Language, in particular, as the primary purveyor of culture and conditions, shapes our cognition about what things *are*, what they are called, and what they mean. But language, words, is always *about* things, their appearance, or how they are represented, rather than what they actually *are*, which is Kant's *Ding-an-sich* or "thing-in-itself." This distinction has been illustrated by expressions such as "the map is not the territory" and "the menu is not the meal . . . so please don't eat the menu." A major question in philosophy since the time of Kant has been how we can get beyond the veil of appearance that our conditioning has imposed upon us.

This question was addressed most directly by the modern school of philosophy known as phenomenology. Although the term phenomenology has been used in a number of different senses, its most common usage is of the movement associated with its founder, Edmund Husserl (1999). In some respects, phenomenology is a method more than a philosophy, although its practice can lead to remarkable philosophical insights, as shown in the works of such moderns as Heidegger, Sartre, and Merleau-Ponty, and also post-moderns, such as Derrida. The method consists of a careful, pre-suppositionless scrutiny of one's consciousness. The essential term in this definition is "presuppositionless," because most of our observations of phenomena are based on our preconceived ideas, theories, or constructions of reality, formed and reinforced by our social conditioning. Thus prejudgment and stereotyping can cloud our direct apprehension of phenomena as they actually are. In the phenomenological method, we are supposed to suspend our opinions, prejudgments, and theories in order to describe what actually *appears*. It is worth noting that the word "phenomenon" derives from *phainesthai*, which is Greek for "to appear." This pure, presuppositionless observation and description of phenomena is very difficult to achieve, and many contemporary philosophers think it is not entirely possible.

Modern science operates very deliberately from preconceived ideas posited by theory. It often derives hypotheses from scientific theories, in order to test them empirically. Phenomenology calls for a very different frame of reference, and the description of phenomena observed through this method requires something like the art of a novelist, in order to yield new and insightful results. In contrast, the results of scientific observation are reported in formulaic style. For this reason, phenomenology has been considered one of the most literary of the modern philosophies.

When the phenomenological method is used in the social and behavioral sciences, it requires that all theories and presuppositions be suspended and "bracketed off" from the observation of the social and behavioral phenomena to be studied and described. This calls for a very intense, careful scrutiny and cleansing of preconceptions, so that the mind is as open as possible to the phenomena as they appear. In this respect, it is very similar to the Eastern practice of mindfulness. In fact, one could say that phenomenology comes closest to the practice of mindfulness of any Western philosophy or discipline.

From the perspective of contemplative psychology, there is a fundamentally different purpose for the methods of phenomenology and those of contemplative practice. For phenomenology, it is to study and describe the observed nature of things, of particular phenomena both mental and physical, for the purpose of advancing knowledge. Philosophy, after all, is the love of knowledge. Although the contemplative practice of meditation is similar to the "bracketing" of preconceptions and opinions to clear the mind, as in the phenomenological method, its purpose is to get beyond the veil of appearance to *experience* the ground and nature of being itself.

It is interesting to look at the work and career of Erich Fromm in this regard. His theoretical training and practice as a psychotherapist was in Freudian psychoanalysis, which he thought, at the time, was a science. Although he was considered something of a Freudian revisionist, like Jung and Adler, his theoretical approach to the study and treatment of psychological disorders was essentially psychoanalytic. However, he also had a philosophical and humanistic dimension to his thinking, and that enabled him to write such widely influential books as *Escape from Freedom* (1941) and *The Sane Society* (1955). Although he began from a strong theoretical base in both his practice and writing, as he entered the latter years of his life, his writing and practice took on a much more contemplative tone, and he turned to the central question of being. His last two books, *To Have or To Be* (1976) and *The Art of Being* (1992), clearly illustrate this.

My own pursuit of a contemplative way of being in old age was heavily influenced by Fromm's example. As a social practitioner myself, I respected him as a practitioner who was also a powerful and innovative social thinker. His approach to the "art" of being was quite applied and down to earth. He not only had a theory or philosophy of being, but he had actual suggestions about how one could go about practicing the art of being. This amounts to *praxis*, a useful term that has a long history in philosophy, going from Aristotle to Kant to Marx and beyond. It has been used interchangeably with *practice*, but it retains its essential meaning of a synthesis of theory and practice. For the purposes of this book, it refers to a seminal theory or philosophy based on the psychological developments of the last stages of life, along with a way or practice for contemplative aging. It can be personified in the life of Fromm. As he moved in his later psychological and philosophical thinking from the issue of having and being to the question of being itself, he found it necessary to have a practice for pursuing the art of being.

In this regard, he was quite emphatic in stating that one of the basic preparations for learning the art is to meditate regularly. The form of meditation he found to be most naturally compatible for a modern Western mind, such as his, was based on the Buddhist concept of mindfulness. He described this as a way of being wherein one is fully concentrated on everything one is doing at any given moment, whether it is planting a seed or cleaning a room or eating. Not only is mindfulness practiced in daily meditation, in which awareness of breathing is the central focus of attention, but from there it can be applied to any moment of daily living. It means *not* doing things in a distracted or routine manner but, rather, applying one's full awareness to such mundane activities as eating, walking, seeing, and thinking, as well as imbuing them with a sense of reverence in the process. This practice amounts to paying attention to the things in their own right, not as a means to some end. The details of this art, or practice, will be presented in a later chapter, but it should be added here that Fromm, like Plotinus, felt that we had to rid ourselves of "having" in order "to be" in its truest sense. While Erich Fromm is an exceptional figure, after all, and cannot easily be emulated as a person by most elders today, his *praxis* can. What is needed is a seminal philosophy or way of being in late life that is both feasible and natural for most elders. Again, this way or style can arise naturally from the normal psychological and physiological developments of later life.

A Natural Philosophy of Age

Perhaps one of the finest and most cogent expressions of this philosophical style was given in the words of Emerson, when he wrote, "It is time to be old, to take in sail . . . [and] . . . timely wise accept the terms . . . . The port, well worth the cruise, is near; and every wave is charmed" (1990, pp. 398-399). Within these few lines, Emerson was able to capture metaphorically the sense of both acceptance and meaning inherent in the philosophical style. Although the lines are from his poem *Terminus*, which deals with finitude, they express something that has had profound meaning for elders over the ages. This is why it has been said in some circles that people become Taoists in their old age. As Taoism was practiced in ancient China, older men and women would, in effect, say, "Now is the time for youth to take over this game of life," and would retire into the mountains to meditate and contemplate nature. There have been a number of lyrical expressions in the Taoist literature of elders going off into the mountains to allow their lives to flow like the mountain streams and float like the mountain clouds.

Other than perhaps going off into the mountains from time to time, what attributes do today's elders have in common with those ancient Chinese elders? The answers lie in the natural physical and psychological developments of old age, and Taoism is a very natural philosophy and way of being in later life. As mentioned earlier, there was a highly influential concept of aging in the field of gerontology called disengagement theory, which claimed, from both a sociological and psychological point of view, that it made sense for elders to disengage from the socioeconomic world, and to allow younger persons to take their places in that world. That theory has since been supplanted, of course, by more activity-oriented conceptions of later life, but it speaks to the universality of the disengagement idea inherent in a number of traditions, most notably Taoism. As an ancient Taoist sage, Chuang Tzu, put it, "Life, then, is really a dream, and we human beings are like travelers floating down the eternal river of time, embarking at a certain point in order to make room for others waiting below the river to come aboard" (see Yutang, 2001, p. 41).

As for the physical developments of old age, it is no accident that the ancient practice of Tai Chi is so popular in senior centers and programs throughout America today. It is a gentle, flowing form of exercise that is compatible with the sinews and joints of the elderly. It maintains fluidity and grace in the aging body, and it has an aesthetic all its own that gives pleasure and contentment in the process. Taoism has been described as the way of nature, destiny, and the cosmos. According to its philosophy, the *Tao* is the source and principle of the cosmic order in which the flow of life force (*chi*) is one of unceasing change. However, the *Tao* is deep, elusive, and obscure, so it cannot be expressed in words. Nevertheless, the *Tao* of humans and that of the universe are one, and therein lays the key to a harmonious human existence in the present. The *Tao Te Ching* is the classic text of Taoist wisdom, and it is almost 2,600 years old, as well as one of the most widely translated and read books in human history. Throughout it, one finds lyrical tributes to simplicity, gentleness and flexibility, living in the present moment, sitting still in silence, moving beyond praise and blame, and seeing the polarities of life in an open and positive way.

The two preeminent Taoist philosophers were Lao Tzu and Chuang Tzu. The former is probably the more widely known of the two because his name is invariably associated with the *Tao Te Ching.* It is not likely Lao Tzu was the sole author of the book, but he was probably its seminal or primary author. Chuang Tzu is, perhaps, the more highly regarded among Western philosophers. Thomas Merton (1965, p.15) wrote, "it would be a great mistake to confuse the Taoism of Chuang Tzu with the popular, degenerate amalgam of superstition, alchemy, magic, and health-culture which Taoism later became." Chuang Tzu's earthy and witty teachings are a pleasure to read, but underneath his humor was a basic percept: "The way of the Tao is to begin with the simple good with which one is endowed by the very fact of existence." Chuang Tzu and Lao Tzu were the major figures in what is known as philosophical Taoism, as opposed to religious or occult Taoism, which has become popularized in America, in terms of a spiritual health culture and esoteric practices. Lao Tzu and Chuang Tzu were philosophers, not shamans. Actually, one of the West's most influential thinkers of the middle and latter half of the twentieth century, Martin Buber, felt that there is a very clear correlation between Greek philosophy and Taoism in the thought of Chuang Tzu, whom he much admired (Herman, 1996). The *Tao*, as understood by Chuang Tzu, and the *Logos*, as understood by Heraclitus, have striking similarities. Everything is flow and change and, for both Chuang Tzu and Heraclitus, it is essential that we understand this and incorporate it fully in our way of life.

The optimal approach to this lifestyle is known in Taoism as *wu-wei*. It means going with the stream, not struggling against the current, and letting the ebbs and tides of one's energy and life force dictate one's actions in harmony with the milieu. *Wu-wei* is not mere inactivity or passivity; it is a knowing and wise activity in which one comprehends the trends of human and natural affairs so well that one uses the least amount of vital energy in dealing with them. It has been called "the innate wisdom of the nervous system," through which one takes the line of least resistance in all one's actions. Now, who more than elders have the experience and the need to practice this wisdom of using one's precious remaining energies with the least resistance and the greatest effect? The process of aging is embraced quite naturally in this philosophy, and it can become an art to go along with the flow of things in a wise and mindful way.

Even meditation is a natural process and not a "discipline" in Taoism. It has been noted that contemplative Taoists will sit happily with yogis and Zazen meditators for as long as it is reasonable and comfortable, but when nature tells them they are "pushing up river" they will get up and do something else, or perhaps go to sleep. Their art is to go along with the flow of things in an intelligent way and, since meditation enhances this kind of intelligence, they engage in the practice. However, their practice is not intended as a form of mind training or discipline as much as it is as a peaceful and pleasurable way of being in itself. Again, in terms of aging, this is consistent with the open, philosophic style Erikson felt was necessary to avoid the "coercive orthodoxy" of the "dogmatic style" of old age. Nevertheless there is a coherent world view and philosophy behind Taoism. It is man's cooperation with the course of the natural world, whose principles we discover most notably in the nonlinear flow patterns of water. For this reason Taoism has been called the "watercourse way" (Watts, 1975).

It is remarkable that Heraclitus (1994) in ancient Greece, a half-planet away from the Taoists, saw the same profound philosophical meanings in the metaphor of flowing water as the Taoists. He is most known for his statement that you cannot step into the same river twice, for new waters are ever flowing in upon you. This is quite consistent with his central doctrine of the flux in all things. He could be called the first formal process philosopher of Western civilization. Process philosophy is an established school of academic philosophy today, and its essential point is that processes are more fundamental than things. There is a long list of Western philosophers in the process tradition, including the likes of Leibniz, Hegel, Bergson, William James, Dewey, and Whitehead. Alfred North Whitehead (1920) adopted "nature as process" as a leading principle, and considered temporality, history, change, and passage as the most fundamental facts we have to deal with in our understanding of the world. We mistake things as solid structures or objects, but the only difference between a structure and a process is that a structure is a much, much slower process than the processes around it, giving it the appearance of solidity. Further, the unity of a thing is a functional unity, a gathering together of a wide variety of energies and moving forces. For John Dewey (1925), a thing is its history; it is a process of many conditions coming together and coming apart, forces cooperating and conflicting.

For William James (1950), the human psyche is a complex of processes, as shown by the affective and cognitive nature of human experience. The stream of consciousness, with its flowing and fusing of mental contents, is consonant with the larger dynamic processes of nature and the universe. And, of course, quantum theory of modern physics (Capra, 2001; Salam & Wigner, 2009; Zukav, 2001) has shown that atoms are not hard and indestructible objects but, rather, at the subatomic level consist of space, in which minute "quanta" move continually and appear at times as particles and then as waves. The theory also reveals a basic oneness of the universe. The phenomenal world cannot be broken down into the smallest conceivable independent units, as was claimed in the earliest atomic theories. So there are no basic isolated building blocks in nature, but something more like a complex web of relations between the various parts of the whole. This web is what Whitehead referred to as the functional unity of the parts to the whole. It would seem, then, that any *natural* philosophy of life and the process of aging would do well to recognize and incorporate these process facts and principles into a praxis and way of being.

The Moral Dimension

The question of what constitutes wisdom in old age has received considerable attention of late in research on aging. There are various ways of addressing the question, but one approach has been to see what attitudes and behaviors of elders are associated with higher morale and life satisfaction. In many instances objective life conditions, such as financial situation, physical health, socioeconomic status, physical environment, and social involvement, do not have as strong a relationship with positive life satisfaction as do the more open, accepting, and compassionate qualities identified largely with contemplative aging. In fact, regret over loss of income, possessions, social status, and social connections are associated with lower life satisfaction. An attitude of caring yet letting go and accepting those losses is directly related to life satisfaction.

These findings point to the advantages of a "being" rather than a "having" orientation, an issue of much concern to Plotinus and Fromm, as noted earlier. This issue also concerned Chuang Tzu, who stated, "He who is controlled by objects loses possession of his inner self." Nevertheless, one of the major problems confronting the older person in our society is "having" a social identity. What is the accepted social identity or image of "old person" in our society? Unlike the very clear and visible identities of younger persons, by virtue of their occupational and parental roles, older persons are left with less salient or definable roles, such as grandparent or "retired person." It cannot be the smiling codger in his golf cap and knickers. Undeniably the social and material losses of the aging self need to be dealt with psychologically and spiritually by older people, or they run the risk of demoralization, and even depression, by virtue of "having" much less than they had when younger. Unfortunately there is an ethos in our society that has exacerbated the problems of lowered self-esteem and loss of identity among older persons, and it has been referred to in the gerontological literature as the "functionalistic ethic" (Bengtson, 1973). This is an ethic by which the person evaluates his or her *self* worth in terms of his or her functional value in society. Since in our society we put the highest premium on the production and consumption of goods and services, the tendency is for the person to be evaluated in terms of productive, professional, or service functioning, monetary worth, and the quantity and quality of goods and services consumed in a market economy. This is not, of course, a very sound standard for self-evaluation by older individuals, who are no longer able to produce or consume in the quantities or style expected by such an ethos. Yet this norm is so ingrained in many of our elders that there is ample empirical evidence to show its negative effects on their morale and life satisfaction.

In a large scale survey of retired men and women in a metropolitan area of the northeastern United States, my colleagues and I found that about one-third of those studied completely identified with and evaluated themselves in terms of the functionalistic ethic (Sherman, 1985). Another twenty per cent primarily identified with it, as measured by their strong agreement with the following survey statements:

1. A person isn't worth much when he or she is no longer able to carry on as a productive member of the community.
2. Unless I feel that I have accomplished or done something that other people value, I feel quite worthless.
3. When you are no longer a contributing member of society by functioning in such roles as worker, parent, etc., you can't really feel that you have value as a person.

Over half of the people sampled strongly agreed with at least two of these tenets of the functionalistic ethic. This was at a serious cost to most of them, because they showed significantly lower scores in measures of self-esteem than the others in the survey. This was particularly the case among those who not only identified with the functionalistic ethic but also identified themselves as less healthy and less competent than others in the sample. Their measures of self-esteem and life satisfaction were among the lowest, and they were a very demoralized group in general. It is clear that an alternative ethos would serve the elderly much better, but it has to be developed and nurtured by the elder himself or herself in a society such as ours. This is why Fromm's emphasis on being rather than having makes sense in later life, and it calls for a contemplative psychology at that stage of life.

The major problem with the functionalistic ethic is that it is widely considered to be the right ethos for the vast majority of older Americans. It assumes, in turn, that when one retires and is no longer an economically productive member of society, one should find a worthwhile alternative function, usually as a "volunteer" in some capacity. The eighteenth century Scottish philosopher David Hume seemed to anticipate this functional imperative when he wrote, "A man who retires from life does no harm to society: He only ceases to do good; which, if it is an injury, is of the lowest kind. All our obligations to do good to society seem to imply something reciprocal. I receive the benefits of society and therefore ought to promote its interests, but when I withdraw myself altogether from society, can I be bound any longer?" (Fingarette, 1996, p. 172). We have already considered the problem this presents to those who are no longer physically able to perform a functional role, but the problem goes well beyond that. Just consider the substantial research findings showing distinct differences in temperament and personality over the life span (McCrae et al., 2000; Sigelman & Rider, 2008). Surely they imply that there is no *one* way to *be* in later life.

Take the example of Henry David Thoreau. He once commented, "As for doing good . . . it does not agree with my constitution." Yet who can say that his writings on human freedom and civil disobedience did not ultimately benefit much of humanity, by influencing later leaders such as Gandhi and Martin Luther King in their non-violent resistance to oppression? The point, however, is not that there was an ultimate benefit to society, but that the functionalistic ethic shoe does not fit all feet. It is a moral philosophy that focuses on what it is right to *do* rather than on what it is good to *be*; it defines the content of obligation rather than the nature of the good life. The medieval German sage and Dominican prior Meister Eckhart once stated, "People never need to think about what they ought to be doing; they should think about what they are" (Van de Weyer, 1998, p. 55). Albert Schweitzer (1947, p. 43) spoke more directly to our current functionalistic society, as follows:

> We do not have enough inwardness, we are not sufficiently preoccupied with our own spiritual life, we lack quietness; and this not only because in our exacting, busy existence it is difficult to obtain, but because, ignoring its importance, we do not take pains to secure it, being too easily contented with living our lives as unrecollected men who merely aim at being good.

The highly socialized view inherent in the functionalistic ethic simply does not allow for the uniqueness of individuals, especially in later life. As James Hillman (1999, p. 37) wrote in *The Force of Character and the Lasting Life*, "we are each an each," and even though we attempt to whittle down the uniqueness and oddities of our individual natures in order to conform during much of our lives, these oddities reemerge and define us in late life. He added, "What one needs blessed are the oddities of character specific to our solitary uniqueness and therefore so hard to bear. I can bless my own virtues, but I need a well-trained, long-suffering eye to bless the virtues concealed in my vices." Hopefully when one reaches old age and has "recollected" oneself through an honest life review, it will become apparent that each of us has elements of the angel and of the devil in our makeup. No one stands beyond good and evil, otherwise that person would not be of this world. Life is a continual balancing of opposing tendencies. This is true of every energic process in life, and the abolition of opposites would be equivalent to the stasis of death.

No one can claim to be moral without coming to a recognition and viable working arrangement between the angel and the devil within. Some of the most dangerous people among us are those who recognize only the angelic side of themselves, and play the role of "good guy" or avenging angel with such blind zeal that the offending other, the "bad guy," has to be wiped out. We see the horrendous results of such thinking in our world today, with all its righteous terrorism and retaliation. As the Russian novelist Alexander Solzhenitsyn, who suffered long incarceration and torture in Soviet gulags, observed in his later life, resolving the moral issue of good and evil would be simple if those people insidiously and invariably committing evil deeds could be separated from the rest of us and destroyed. But, as he added, the dividing line between good and evil "cuts through the heart" of every human being.

The visionary poet and artist William Blake insisted on the inescapability of both good and evil in life. In *The Marriage of Heaven and Hell*, completed around 1790, he claimed the necessity of their co-present oppositions in his famous statement: "Without contraries is no progression." This expresses one of the highest aims in the spiritual traditions of the East, to realize that good and bad, pleasure and pain, birth and death are two sides of the same reality, not two absolutely opposite self-contained categories of human experience. There is an actual mutuality of opposites, and their polar relationship is, in fact, a unity. This correlative vision is a precious insight in later life, as one deals with the remembrances and regrets of past behaviors and relationships. The fact is that no two opposites can exist unless there is a relationship between them. This is inherent even in the very structure of human language, as Jacques Derrida recognized when he stated in *Of Grammatology* (1997), "the privileged term is *constituted* by what it suppresses." The moralistic protagonist's rhetoric is propelled by the opposite suppressed or repressed impulses within him or her.

This was inherent in a fundamental principle upon which ancient Chinese thought developed, and it is none other than the principle of the *yin* and the *yang,* which is at the heart of Taoism. On this view, the universe is made up of primordial opposites such as *hot* and *cold, male* and *female*, and, of course, *positive* and *negative*. The key idea here is that through differences, and through differences in every variety, an overriding and encompassing unity is discovered. Differences are really two sides of a thing, and you can't have one side without the other, which is why, from an encompassing view, they become inseparably one. One of the highest aims of the spiritual tradition of the East is the awareness that all opposites are polar and inextricably form a unity. To return to the moral theme of the positive and the negative, or the good and the bad, it can be seen that a transcendent or encompassing view is necessary to come to terms with the primordial reality of difference, which is ultimately subsumed within the One. Perhaps saints appear to be pursuing the totally positive and the absolutely good, but the way of Taoist philosophy is that of the sage and not the saint. Neither Lao Tzu nor Chuang Tzu ever claimed any saintly aspirations, nor would any wise elder, to my knowledge. So the natural and contemplative philosophy of age is in the direction of wisdom, not saintliness.

We moderns are in need of a new and different awareness of evil, to recognize its emergence within ourselves. This is the "dark" side, the shadow part of our personalities, as Jung put it. This side has too often been seen as outside ourselves, projected onto other persons and nations, so as to find a scapegoat for our own negative impulses and shortcomings. An awareness of both positive and negative forces within the individual and the collective has become necessary for our survival in the twenty-first century. For the individual, this awareness can provide for a humane moral attitude toward oneself and others in later life. Such awareness requires a broad, comprehensive philosophical and experiential view, a meta-perspective, which Jaspers called the *Encompassing*, Plotinus called the *One*, and Tornstam called *Gerotranscendence*.

Chapter Three

The Aging Self

Soren Kierkegaard, the prolific nineteenth century philosopher and theologian, once observed that life is lived forward and understood backward. Actually, there is good reason to believe that this reality accounts for the increase in the frequency of reminiscence that we find among older people. It is consistent with a widely held theory in gerontology, that increased reminiscence is a natural psychological development in the later part of life (usually in our sixties and seventies), in order to review one's life, and put it in perspective in preparation for death. Much of this is directed toward trying to understand just who one has been for most of one's life. Yet there is evidence from gerontological research and practice that seems to indicate most of the increased reminiscence is not consciously directed toward a life review or self-understanding.

Remembering and Reviewing

Studies indicate that a relatively small proportion (fifteen to twenty percent) of individuals aged sixty and over report finding themselves reminiscing as a way to understand themselves and their lives (Romaniuk & Romaniuk, 1981; Sherman, 1991). The large majority report that they engage in reminiscence because it provides pleasure and lifts their spirits. They enjoy it because it offers the opportunity to talk about or think about the interesting, humorous, or touching events and experiences of their lives. There is usually a "good old days" feel about it when it goes on in groups, although not always. There is often talk about how "tough" things were in the past and people would "make do," yet it is evident that talking about these less pleasant things from the past gives pleasure in the present. Although this type of reminiscing will not lead to a Kierkegaardian understanding of life, there is nothing problematic about it in terms of gerontological practice. Actually, it is generally associated with high measures of self-reported well-being and morale. The more frequently people engage in this kind of reminiscence, the higher their morale and life-satisfaction scores on certain psychological measures, such as the Life Satisfaction Index (Neugarten, Havighurst, & Tobin, 1961). Consequently, such reminiscence is encouraged and elicited by most practitioners in their work with aged individuals and groups. Sharing similar memories of this pleasant sort is one of the most effective social "ice breakers" among older people who do not know one another, and this is why memory-sharing groups are so popular and commonly found in senior centers and nursing homes throughout the United States.

Yet even when reminiscing goes on in private and alone, rather than with others, it is generally not directed toward the understanding of life or the self. There are three rather distinct forms or uses of reminiscence that are involved in a true life review: (1) to resolve something from the past that is troubling the person, (2) to arrive at a better understanding of one's self, and (3) to determine the meaning of one's life. Not surprisingly, these life review forms have been referred to collectively as "existential/self-understanding" reminiscence, but as noted earlier, only about one in five elders report having engaged in all three forms (Romaniuk & Romaniuk, 1981; Sherman & Peak, 1991). If they had, such a life review process should lead to what Erik Erikson (1968) has called an *existential* identity, which differs significantly from his famous concept of *ego* identity. He saw the developmental task of adolescence as searching for, finding, and then enacting the social roles we take to be our personal identities within society and the larger culture. Youth needs to pursue a sense of self, an ego identity, against a countervailing sense of "ego diffusion" and "role confusion." The task is to determine who one is within the social scheme of things, as well as what one is to become. An analogous task faces us in later life, with the advent of retirement and the loss of the major social roles that define identity within society. What is one's identity then? Presumably we can find it through the life review process. As Erikson saw it, there needs to be an evaluation and modification of the personal system of behaviors, values, and beliefs that exemplify the self in later life. Through the life review process, elders modify their philosophies of life, so as to correspond more to the lives they have actually lived. Thus, existential identity deals more with the core elements of the person's character and beliefs than with appearances and the person's social persona.

Autobiographical Consciousness

An existential life review process calls for a certain kind of consciousness, which I think was most appropriately named and defined as "autobiographical consciousness" by William Earle (1972), a professor of philosophy for many years at Northwestern University, until his death in 1988. He defined autobiographical consciousness in terms of Socrates' famous dictum, "Know thyself," which means I have "to become explicit as to who I am, what it is for me to exist, what my *singular* existence has been, where it is now, and what lies before me" (Earle, 1972, p. 10). This kind of knowing is not explanatory but, instead, involves raising to explicit consciousness that which is already implicitly known. Although this sort of knowledge may be implicitly grasped, there is no guarantee, or even likelihood, that it will be elucidated and made explicit to any great extent, in what Earle called one's "ontological autobiography." In fact, there are certain aspects of autobiographical consciousness that might lead many elders *not* to raise this knowledge to explicit consciousness; and it is this that leads to the problems to be discussed in this chapter. They are not problems of memory or memory deficit, such as Alzheimer's disease, another form of dementia, or even the marginal memory losses found in normal aging. In fact, what cognitive psychologists call "autobiographical memory" remains remarkably strong and resilient into very old age (Bolles, 1988). So it is not cognitive or memory deficits that are problematic in this regard. It is that the kind of self and life examination called for by autobiographical consciousness is often avoided or circumscribed, because of the negative, often painful, memories and emotions evoked by it.

Past traumas, losses, transgressions, regrets, and so on, are frequently the problematic content of this consciousness. Sometimes this failure of attention to lived experience and significant autobiographical content is an indication of a reactive depression, the most common psychiatric problem found among the elderly. In other instances, the problem is that the older person is stuck on some particular issue or event in the past, and cannot get beyond it into other areas that could provide meaning and understanding about the person's life. This amounts to morbid rumination rather than benign or positive reminiscence, since compulsively going over the same issue *ad infinitum* leads to continual feelings of guilt, regret, shame, and other negative emotions that become progressively demoralizing and depleting in their effects. Consequently, there are strong, even sound, motives for not engaging in an authentic life review.

In a sense, one could say that these people are "in flight" from such remembering and self understanding, as Heidegger would put it. These are some of the more serious problems associated with autobiographical consciousness, but there are others of importance. So much of the autobiographical reminiscence that goes on in later life is lacking in rich and meaningful memorial content. Many of the truly significant events and experiences are overlooked, bypassed, circumvented, denied, or repressed. Also, the recollections and memories that *are* brought forth are without depth or density, and there appears to be a lack of awareness or insight in what is recalled. The problem with such recollection is that many people bypass their last opportunity for an examined life, which Socrates claimed was the only life worth living. In addition, they are bypassing a rich and sustaining resource for well-being, creativity, and meaning in their remaining years.

I have interviewed and worked with older individuals with very troubled backgrounds, as well as humble origins, education, and vocation, who still possess a remarkably rich, knowing, and sustaining kind of autobiographical consciousness in later life. Regardless of their level of education or verbal facility, their life narratives were remarkably reflective and even inspired.

Knowing One's Self

Socrates was not the only ancient Greek thinker to take the Delphic commandment of "Know Thyself" to heart. He was preceded in this by Heraclitus of Ephesus (1994), who not only advocated knowing one's self, but added that one should then *become* that self. Heraclitus also maintained that character is destiny, and, presumably, if one knows one's self (one's character) it is possible to live out one's destiny in full consciousness, rather than to be buffeted by fate in a fog of unknowingness. This Greek view of the self changed with the advent and dominance of Christianity in the West, according to which the person was seen as part of a system of hierarchical levels of being with God at the apex. In the Middle Ages, each person had his or her place, role, and identity within a larger socio-religious system. This system gave way during the Renaissance and Reformation with the onslaught of empiricism and the arrival of the Enlightenment, in the early eighteenth century. This philosophy stressed practical improvement over theoretical or metaphysical speculation, and it developed concepts of the self that were suited to a growing individualism and reliance on reason, rather than on religious belief and orthodoxy.

These concepts of the self tended to fall into two major groupings. One grouping claimed an inner core of authentic selfhood, in which the individual should seek to gain access to that true self and be faithful to it. This, in a sense, is a return to the ancient Greek views of Socrates and Heraclitus, resulting from the growing emphasis on the individual during the Enlightenment. The other grouping claimed that the self is socially conditioned, and is nothing more than a series of social roles we play. These two groupings have been referred to, respectively, as the "onion" and the "artichoke" views of the self. On the onion view, as you continue to strip off the outer layers of self you find there is no inner core. In the case of the artichoke, you do indeed come upon an inner core after stripping off the outer layers. These two views are still prevalent, and psychologists and sociologists currently tend to favor one or the other way of thinking about the self.

The artichoke idea of an innate self has been proposed by various psychologists, notably James Hillman (1999), who, in his "acorn theory," claims that "each person bears a uniqueness that asks to be lived and that is already present before it can be lived." This is in the form of a primal image of the character with which we are born and that will shape our destinies; it is a given and a gift. Hillman claims, as did Socrates, that one's uniqueness would be known through one's *daimon*, which is an inner guide and carrier of one's destiny that knows the image and pattern of the life one will live on earth. Thus to become one's self is to know and follow the guidance of one's daimon. This should not be taken as an arcane issue from ancient thought or mythology, for there has been an enduring question in modern psychology as to whether the self, as character or personality, is something largely constitutional and inborn or something determined and constructed in and by the environment and social interaction in the course of life. In philosophy, this same issue has been posed in terms of a *created* versus a *discovered* self. The "Know Thyself" of Socrates and Heraclitus was clearly referring to a self that could be discovered, or, for Socrates, to be remembered in anamnesis.

In the modern era, existentialist philosophers, such as Jean-Paul Sartre, were opposed to the idea of an essence, an "essential" self of an inborn nature. For him, the self is created in action and interaction, and in this sense we create our own identities. From Sartre's point of view, we are free to choose what we will be as this is manifested in our actions, beliefs, and attitudes in the lived world. But it is revealing that Sartre was not able to sustain this belief in its pure form into his old age. In his later years, as he was working on his biographical study of Gustave Flaubert (Sartre, 1993), he became fascinated with Flaubert's uniqueness as a person and a writer. When he was asked whether Flaubert had demonstrated this existential freedom of self-creation in his life, Sartre replied, "Flaubert was free to be Flaubert but not free to be someone else." This certainly suggests that Sartre came to the conclusion that there was an essential Flaubert whose destiny could only be realized in his life in terms of his inborn and predetermined potentiality. Thus, Flaubert was free to actualize this potentiality in his life, or not, but nothing else could be authentic for him. This view represented a return on Sartre's part to classical realistic philosophy, which held that one has the choice of fulfilling one's nature or not, but that one could not create another destiny.

What is the empirical evidence regarding this nature versus nurture controversy in contemporary psychology? Most of the modern research (Damon, Lerner & Eisenberg, 2006; Turunen, 2008; Wilson & Matheny, 1983) on the subject of human temperament done by experts on infant and child development and comparative studies of twins raised in different environments, plus research findings from neuroscience and the biochemistry of the brain, agree on four criteria that define temperament: (1) it appears early in life, (2) it has some genetic basis, (3) it varies among individuals, and (4) it generally shows stability over time and situations. The recent research findings show that it is a combination of inherited physiology plus experience that makes for a certain kind of temperament and character. People who inherit certain bio-psychological tendencies will gravitate toward experiences that will reinforce those very traits, but that does not mean that the genetic tendency has to remain rigidly fixed or highly predictable. Genes seem to affect the mind somewhat indirectly, by leaning toward formative experiences. However, the idea that early experience in the home, particularly in the nuclear family, determines most of the personality has been seriously weakened by recent findings. Hillman (1996) refers to this as "the family fallacy." The empirical fact that siblings do not demonstrate personalities that are more similar to one another than those of unrelated children suggests that, although the family has half its genes in common, it does not even out the differences among siblings in any significant way. Most telling is the research done on identical twins reared separately from birth (Farber, 1981; MCTFR, 2010; Mysteries of Twins, 1998). These pairs are not only remarkably alike in IQ, boldness, inhibition, and aggressiveness, but in specific things, such as the way two sisters who have never met one another count themselves to sleep. Small, utterly unique, features such as these abound in anecdotes from the research on twins.

One of the pre-eminent developmental psychologists and researchers on human temperament, Jerome Kagan of Harvard, reports that early in his career he began with a bias toward nurture rather than nature, because of his training, politics, and values. He was not alone in this; it was the prevalent view among developmental psychologists thirty years ago. He felt that the environment, especially the family in early childhood, was much more determining of personality or character than one's biological type and innate temperament based on neuro-chemistry. He finally had to admit, "I have been dragged, kicking and screaming, by my data to acknowledge that temperament is more powerful than I thought and wish to believe." His highly informative book on the subject, *Galen's Prophecy: Temperament in Human Nature* (Kagan, 1994), traces the concept of innate dispositions and temperaments from the time of Galen, a remarkably perceptive second-century Greek physician, to the present. Galen identified four temperamental categories based on the "humors" of the body: melancholic (sad), sanguine (cheerful), choleric (angry), and phlegmatic (cool and self-possessed).

In the modern era, some psychological research has demonstrated the considerable explanatory power of Galen's categories (Eysenck & Eysenck, 1985; Kagan, 1994). However, this research reframes the Galenic concepts in a way that enhances their explanatory value by positing the distinction made by Jung between *introverts* and *extraverts*. The reason for adding this dimension is that introversion/extraversion has been found to be a largely inborn dimension of personality (Bienvenu et al., 2007; Scarr, 1969). It has to be taken into account in any consideration of character and self because it has life-long effects and implications. There is some similarity between Galen's melancholic and introverted types. For example the introvert has a tendency to withdraw from social interaction, to avoid conflict, to be cautious in risky situations, and to engage in solitary activities. Extraverts have similarities with Galen's sanguine type, in that they enjoy sociability, like excitement, and show a more carefree, spontaneous, and even impulsive style. However, the matter is more complex than that, because further research (Eysenck's Personality Inventory, 2010) has found a stable/unstable dimension to both introversion and extraversion, so the resulting framework now identifies different types of personality with considerable clinical specificity on the basis of the four resulting categories of *extraverted/stable, extraverted/unstable, introverted/stable,* and *introverted/unstable*. For example, male criminals tend to be unstable extraverts, as do sociopathic individuals, whereas obsessional neurotics and persons with general anxiety states tend to be unstable introverts. They certainly fit in Galen's melancholic category. On the other hand, stable introverts tend to be passive, carefree, thoughtful, peaceful, controlled, reliable, even tempered, and calm—traits that are much more consistent with Galen's sanguine type. Their stable extraverted counterparts are sociable, outgoing, talkative, responsive, easygoing, lively, and drawn to leadership— traits that are certainly sanguine.

Research in this area also finds that introverts let in much more stimuli by way of their nervous systems and seem preoccupied by its internalization. What psychologists have found through questionnaire and interview survey methods appears markedly similar to what neuroscientists have been discovering through brain imaging technology. Without becoming too technical, what these researchers have found is that introverts are connected with the acetylcholine, or energy conserving, parasympathetic nervous system, whereas extraverts are connected with the dopamine/adrenaline, energy spending, and sympathetic nervous system. On PET scans, introverts show increased activity in the frontal lobes of the brain as well as the front thalamus, which are areas associated with internal processing. Extraverts show increased activity in areas connected with sensory processing, in the back thalamus and temporal lobes, which is indicative of the extravert's need for sensory stimulation and activity from the outside. Since the introvert's brain focuses on inward processing, the introvert feels energized through introspection, recalling, planning, and complex thinking, all of which seem compatible with a reflective and perhaps contemplative frame of mind.

Extraverts, on the other hand, tend to be energetic, active and stimulated by activity, readily get into the middle of things, and like variety rather than sameness. They usually have many friends and enjoy talking, even with strangers, often talk or act without needing to think first, and tend to talk more than listen. These traits are more consistent with the active than the contemplative life. Conversely, introverts talk less and listen more, although they can talk at length about subjects they consider important. They also tend to think before speaking or acting, and have difficulty thinking and responding when in groups or high-pressure situations. They have relatively few friends but they have deep friendships, and they prefer to relax alone or with a few close friends. They are generally calm, self-contained, prefer to observe than be in the middle of things, and feel the need to rest after engaging in outside activities, even those activities they enjoy. This is not the American norm. As Kagan (1994, p. 29) wrote in *Galen's Prophecy*, "American society is suspicious of the introverted isolate with one or two friends who avoid social gatherings. Immanuel Kant would have been surprised by this contemporary prejudice. He was of the opinion that 'separation from all society is regarded as sublime. . . . To be sufficient for oneself, and consequently to have no need of society, without at the same time being unsociable, is something bordering on the sublime'." Kant, after all, was a classic introvert, but was able to live a highly reflective solitary kind of life as a lifelong bachelor in Konigsberg, Prussia, where he was born and never left. He taught at the university there for most of his adult life, in the latter part of the eighteenth century, and since he was financially secure, he was able to live a hermetic existence that suited his character perfectly. His contemplative aging was certainly enhanced by his introverted personality. However, simply being born an introvert is no guarantee of living a contemplative old age, as indicated by the earlier description of the unstable introverted personality.

Such differences in temperament have shown remarkable consistency in longitudinal and age-comparative research on change and continuity in personality over the life span into very late life. Different types of personality measurement procedures have shown personality to be quite stable, especially after age thirty, throughout the remainder of the life cycle (Atchley, 1999; Sigelman & Rider, 2008).

What does this have to say about a contemplative versus an active life style in old age? It would seem that the personality characteristics of a lifelong extravert would not incline that individual toward a contemplative old age. Such a person would be inclined to live the *vita activa* as long as possible, and rightly so. It would seem that the person with the introverted-stable personality would be most inclined toward the contemplative style. Yet both introverts and extraverts can achieve and enhance a more contemplative existence in later life through a number of mindful and meditative practices, which are spelled out in Chapter Five.

Becoming One's Self

George Santayana, the Spanish philosopher, poet, essayist, and novelist, once remarked that when we are too old to *do* we become what we *are*. That is, we can become what it is in our nature to be. Aristotle claimed that things as well as persons should become what they were meant to be, to become what is intrinsically right for them, and he called this process *entelechy*. Buddhist philosophy is quite the opposite; it clearly takes the onion view of the self, and asserts there is no unique individual self when you "peel away the layers." It (the self) is a mistaken mental and social construction and, therefore, an illusion. The concept of *anata*, or no-self, is central to its teaching. The more ancient Taoist view is less obvious and, perhaps, paradoxical on this point, as is true of its philosophy in general. In the *Tao Te Ching*, it is written that he who knows others is wise, and he who knows himself is enlightened. This seems to imply that there is an actual self to know. Yet there is a further Taoist statement that advises us to first have the strength to meet the self and then have the strength to let go of the self. When applied to elders, this could be taken to mean having the strength to go through an existential life review, as described earlier, but in the process letting go of the conceits, regrets, and concerns that make up our ego selves. Having the strength to let go of the ego self makes considerable sense in late life, when considered in the light of William James's process conception of the self and its fateful trajectory in the human life cycle.

James conceived of the self as duplex, i.e., consisting of self-as-subject (I) and self-as-object (Me). He wrote,

> Whatever I may be thinking of, I am always at the same time more or less aware of *myself*, of my *personal existence*. At the same time it is *I* who am aware; so that the total self of me, being as it were duplex, partly known and partly knower, partly object and partly subject, must have two aspects discriminated in it, of which for shortness we may call one the *Me* and the other the *I*. (James, 1985, p. 43)

It is the *Me* that I and others can most readily identify as our "self," because it is the more observable and describable self. The *I* is the observing, but non-observable and subjective, aspect of the self. Because of its more observable and known nature, James focused mostly on the empirical self, the *Me*. He identified three basic constituents of the *Me:* (1) the material, (2) the social, and (3) the spiritual. The body is the innermost part of the "material *Me*." Our body image is central to our self-image; it is what we see, imagine, and remember ourselves to be. Thus, the clothes that adorn our bodies are closely associated with the material *Me*, and all things intimately associated with both the material and the social *Me* are seen as "mine." Therefore, my family, spouse, children, friends, home, and my other possessions are all experienced as mine, and as extensions of *Me*. They are basic parts of my assumptive world and any diminishment or loss of any of them is experienced as a diminishment of me. The decrements and losses that naturally occur in late life have their effects on the nature of the aging self.

It needs to be emphasized here that the *I* and the *Me* are in a constant dynamic and inseparable relationship with one another, and are really two aspects of the same *process*, i.e., the ever-changing yet continuous self as revealed in our stream of consciousness. On this view, the *I* is continually conscious of the thoughts, feelings, and actions of the self through time and the lived life. Yet these experiences of the self in the past are retained and remembered only as part of the known self, the *Me*, because the material and social aspects of the *Me* are much more apparent and "objective" to us than the spiritual aspect. What can be more concretely known to us than our own bodies, clothing, possessions, families, and friends?

The spiritual *Me* is much less obvious. However, James identified it as "the entire collection of my states of consciousness, my psychic faculties and disposition. . . ." He added, "The more *active-feeling* states of consciousness are the . . . more central portion of the spiritual *Me*. The very core and nucleus of our self, as we know it, the very sanctuary of our life, is the sense of activity which certain inner states possess" (James, 1985, p. 48). Although this aspect of the *Me* is much less obvious than the material and social aspects, it marks the direction in which the process of interiority proceeds in later life. We go in that direction to find the core values and meaning in our lives, our essential self.

Figure 1, which resembles what is called the Normal Curve in statistics, is a crude portrayal of the kind of process the known self (the Jamesian *Me*) undergoes in the course of aging. There is a trajectory of ascent and growth from birth to around age fifty, where it frequently peaks in terms of the accumulation of the social and material aspects of self (friends, family, wealth, property, etc.), and is, therefore, represented as the largest area beneath the curve. This is a curve that is every bit as "normal" in aging as it is in statistics. As the self approaches death along the trajectory, the spiritual dimension becomes proportionally more prominent and significant, and the social and material dimensions become less prominent.

Figure 1

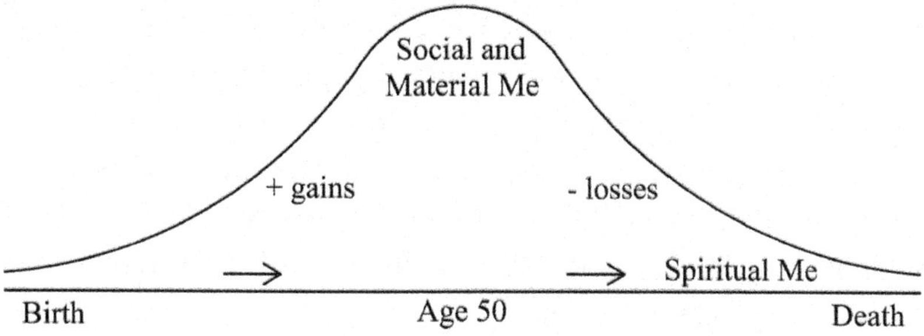

This spiritual process would seem to be a natural and, perhaps, wise reaction to fact that there will be losses and decrements in the material and social dimensions of our lives and selves, such as a deteriorating body, the loss of loved ones, and so on. A former academic colleague once remarked that we seem to spend half of our lives finding our place in the world, finding our sexual orientation, our appointed work, the things and people that help or hinder us along our way. But toward the middle, around fifty or so, we change direction and seek knowledge of the world and mankind and, especially, knowledge of ourselves. Although he was not religious, my colleague surmised that this is what is probably meant by the expression "we make up our souls," in the spiritual sense. However, there are different ways of handling the reality of this trajectory. Those who have not contemplated or prepared for its decrements and finitude might use the psychological defense of denial to evade the realization of their inevitability, but that will not work well, because the losses along the way are too obvious and too painful. The perspective that is most suited to sustaining morale and meaning in later life is an orientation of "being" rather than "having." As noted earlier, Erich Fromm felt that the distinction between these two orientations or modes of existence was of critical importance. He described the having orientation as follows: "In the having mode of existence my relationship to the world is one of possessing and owning, one in which I want to make everybody and everything, including myself, my property" (Fromm, 1976, p. 24). In the being mode, life is experienced as a process rather than a property, and is characterized by acceptance of change and an attitude of caring non-attachment, rather than possessiveness.

Applying this distinction to the Jamesian concept of the self in the course of aging, the material and social *Me* both have strong proprietary elements identified by the possessive terms "my" or "mine." The aging person with a strong having orientation is going to experience great difficulty in a vain attempt to hold on to those objects and persons, which are internalized as extensions of the self through regressive and possessive memory. For this reason, it is sometimes said that the capacity for gently "letting go" is a true asset in later life, and it is more characteristic of a being than a having orientation.

However, there is more to the being orientation than letting go; it includes a capacity for creating or bringing about something qualitatively different in response to what has been lost. According to James, the generative capacities of the *Me* lie much more in its spiritual dimension than in the material or the social dimensions, because the states of consciousness and psychic faculties that include thought, emotion, and imagination are most active there. That is where the vital pattern of later life is to be found and experienced, often in a very creative way.

This is tellingly portrayed in the aging experience of the revered German graphic artist and sculptor Kathe Kollwitz. Her superb woodcuts and lithographs of families, particularly mothers and children, attest to her devotion to family and loved ones, in both her life and her art. However, in later life she found familial ties growing looser. She wrote that for the last third of her life there remained only her work as an artist. Her increased interiority carried her further into the creative core of her being, as the attachment to others loosened through losses and the passage of time. Yet it is clear that her creative later life was informed by powerful inner images of family, such as the anguished portrayal conveyed in her 1910 etching titled "Death and the Mother." Although there was detachment, there was love and a profound creative caring. In a lighter vein, James described the process of detachment and letting go with a sense of relief, as follows: "How pleasant is the day when we give up striving to be young,—or slender! Thank God! we say, *those* illusions are gone. Everything added to the Self is a burden as well as a pride" (1985, p. 54).

The spiritual *Me* of the Jamesian self can be viewed as that aspect of the mortal self that is transitional toward a greater, more sacred Self. This could be likened to the *Atman* in the Vedic tradition, the *Ruh* in Sufism, or the *Ein Sof* in the Kabbalah tradition of Judaism. From another perspective, the *I* of James's duplex self can be viewed as the transcendental aspect of the self. Wittgenstein once exclaimed, "The I, the I is what is deeply mysterious." He illustrated this graphically by drawing a picture of the human eye and noting that this is not what we see when we look. It is the observing but not the observable, and this is held as supremely transcendent in the Buddhist tradition. It has the potential to be the centerpiece or the cosmic consciousness of gerotranscendence for many elders. Erikson (1986, p. 52) observed that it takes a sense of "I" to be aware of a "myself," or a series of myselves over time to retain a feeling of continuity in personal identity. He added that "the 'I', after all, is the ground for the simple verbal assurance that each person is a center of awareness in a universe of communicable experience, a center so numinous that it amounts to a sense of being alive and, more, of being the vital condition of existence." He felt, also, that the sense of "I" in old age provided "a once-for-all chance of transcending time-bound identities." This is very close to James's conception of the "*I*" in relation to the "spiritual *Me*."

But if we return to the more earth-bound conception of the spiritual *Me*, with its core values and attitudes, we recognize that the later part of life is not always an easy one, especially for the very old. They have lost partners, friends, family, even children, who shared with them a common world, a social and historical context about which they could talk and commune in mutual understanding. Their world of common experience and acquaintances has disintegrated, so that the process of becoming in very late life is one of isolation and estrangement from the world. What kind of fulfillment in terms of becoming oneself is possible in this process of loss and personal diminishment? Paradoxically, the very process of loss and diminishment can be an enlightening experience in itself. Prior illusions about unlimited hopes and possibilities in becoming can now be seen in the clear light of finitude. This experience of limitedness allows us to understand our lives as forming a unique and singular totality, which is a true becoming of one's self. Thus, old age is a time of life in which fulfillment and limitedness are truly understood in the crossing of finitude and meaning. This consciousness of time and meaning, of the limitations and vulnerability of being human, teaches us the value of slowness, of pausing, of calm attention and reflection on past and present. It takes such a calm looking backward, a contemplation of the full life span that enables us to achieve an emancipated clarification of life. It allows one to focus on contentment and fulfillment in the present, providing the sense of an eternal now, rather than pining for happiness in the future or hoarding it from the past. The opportunity for a modest, non-egoistic sense of happiness and fulfillment is in many ways unparalleled in old age.

If one understands the process of becoming-a-self in its finality, it can lead to a more conscious life. Thus, as Aristotle claimed, we can agree that true, constant happiness is based on this insight. There is another aspect to this potential for grace and happiness, and it has to do with the diminishment of the material and social aspects of the self, the *Me*. In the total process of finally coming to know oneself and then becoming that self, one has followed this wise ancient adage: "First have the strength to meet the self; then have the strength to let go of the self." It is not a complete and abrupt letting-go, but rather a gradual release and lightening of the spirit. This lightness is the opposite of heavy darkness, so one can truly find the "lightness of being" to be bearable, contra Kundera. As Chesterton once noted, "The reason angels can fly is that they have learned to take themselves lightly."

Perhaps the greatest feeling of lightness and transcendence in the mere fact of being is provided by the recognition and reflection upon the fact that our core sense of self, the I, is located in awareness itself and not in its mental contents. Awareness is the field in which all these contents exist and is the ground of conscious life, the ground of being. The body, the self-image, and the self-concept are all mental constructs that we observe in that awareness. The innermost self is the ground of consciousness that reflects all those contents like a mirror. Potentially, it is the greatest gift and resource in later life, if one attends to and reflects upon it with regularity into a contemplative old age.

Being One's Self

If we view the *I-Me* self as a process rather than an entity, it implies ongoing change of the self even into very old age. Given that there is such change, is there any evidence of continuity of character and personality in the self during later life? The evidence is very strong in gerontological research that there is continuity in personality, particularly in characteristic traits and behaviors, as noted earlier. The overall research evidence is such that "continuity theory" (Atchley, 1999) is one of the most highly regarded and explanatory theories in gerontology today. It holds that there is significant continuity of patterns of thought and behavior throughout the adult life cycle; and they endure over time, in large part, because they are the result of selective investments of time and energy in preferred personal goals and activities. At the same time, the theory is about adaptation. Individuals not only make choices to achieve preferred goals, but they have to adapt to constantly changing circumstances in doing so. This makes the theory commensurable with a process conception of aging. It is also pluralistic in the Jamesian sense that there is no one preferred lifestyle or pattern that leads to successful aging. This would seem to be the case because successful elders appear to have selected lifestyles that fit their own unique personalities and life goals.

So, rather than a no-change concept of continuity, the theory is dynamic and evolutionary, in that it sees recurring themes and persistent patterns, in which the details change but the basic pattern is maintained. If one thinks of the literary concept of continuity, in which there is continuity of character, this evolutionary aspect is quite clear. It is not that nothing happens to a character in a story or a literary narrative, but, rather, that the character remains recognizably unique over the course of the narrative. James Hillman (1999), from his perspective of archetypal psychology, makes this literary conception of uniqueness in old age abundantly clear in his book *The Force of Character and the Lasting Life*. In it, he claims that the last years of life confirm and fulfill character. Although Heraclitus was a process philosopher, he believed that character is destiny, and it is never more destined than in old age. For Hillman, character is equated with soul, but very much an embodied soul. He puts it this way (1999, p. 7):

> Character! Character governs—governing physiology, too. We will be maintaining (in old age), with all the heft and perseverance we can still summon, that genetic inheritance is shaped into our peculiar pattern by character. That specific composition of traits, foibles, delights, and commitments, that identifiable figure bearing our name, our history, and a face that mirrors a 'me'.

He goes on to say that our bodies and our minds cannot avoid change, but what remains is that enduring psychological component called character, which marks one as a being different from all others. We can lose our social identities and our physical configurations, but something will outlast these real vicissitudes of old age, and that is character, the lasting core of self. This core is very much what William James meant by the "Spiritual *Me*." However, this concept of soul is not to be taken as "good" in the moral sense. To be unique as a character is to be odd, atypical, and different. The integrity of character asks only that "one be what one is and nothing more or other," according to Hillman.

As a psychologist with a strong literary background, Hillman has an appreciation of what creative literature can provide in the way of human insights; and one of America's greatest men of letters, Ralph Waldo Emerson, wrote eloquently of the lasting strength and call of character. He noted that each one of us has a certain form of living, speaking, and behaving that are independent of the will, but wholly dependent on one's character and condition. His hope was to end alienation by reconciling the person with his or her own essence, as he tried so successfully to do in his famous essay "Self-Reliance" (1981). What do we mean here by "essence"? Spinoza, the seventeenth century Dutch philosopher, defined it as "The endeavor to persist in its own being." This suits Emerson's meaning very well. It should be added that Emerson also observed that each of us has to "contemplate his own proper nature." That is good advice for later life and undertaking a life review.

Character and self, of course, require an autobiographical consciousness, and no man of letters captured the nature of this consciousness in later life better than Tolstoy, as may be seen in the following quotation by Robert Butler (1970, p. 125), the eminent gero-psychiatrist and Pulitzer Prize-winning author: "I remember very vividly that I am conscious of myself in exactly the same way now, at 81, as I was conscious of myself, my 'I' at five or six years of age. Consciousness is immovable. Due to this alone there is a movement which we call 'time.' If time moves on, there must be something that stands still; the consciousness of my 'I' stands still."

Tolstoy's "I" is very much the "I" of William James's duplex self. The "Me," with all its physical and social components may deteriorate or pass away, but the "I" remains. This is indeed a continuing feature of the self.

Chapter Four

A Contemplative Way

There are many ways of being contemplative. For example, there is the way of the monk whose contemplation consists primarily of prayer and meditation on sacred matters and duties. Or there is the way of the philosopher, such as Immanuel Kant, whose contemplation is essentially on matters metaphysical, epistemological, and moral. And there are numerous other ways in different cultures, settings, and persons. One would assume that most elders would be contemplative to the extent of reviewing their past, in an attempt to see what meaning or place their lives might have in the overall scheme of things (Butler, 1963). But as shown in Chapter Three, it appears that most do not engage in such a review. Some gerontologists who have studied this phenomenon were perplexed by the fact that such individuals may even transform potentially deep questions of the meaning of existence into relatively trivial, mundane matters, such as to whom to leave the family silver. Perhaps for many elders those existential questions have been answered by the religions or belief systems into to which they were born or came to believe. Perhaps others have never had the inclination to engage such questions because they have always felt too engaged in meeting the contingencies of their lives and living out each day. In this sense, they have not taken the time to develop the frame of mind that would lead them to become contemplative in later life.

The Experiential Dimension

The natural development of interiority and the fact of retirement together allow for a contemplative way of being in later life. If the individual chooses to go this way, it involves a shift to a more receptive and allowing mode of being, and away from one of forced and willful action. For some this would represent an almost seismic shift in consciousness, but it is one that occurs gradually rather than abruptly in the aging process. To say that one chooses to go this way is not quite accurate, for in my experience it involves a feeling of being drawn in that direction, and it is more in the nature of an inclination or a call. For many elders, this may be a siren's call to be resisted and, instead, to redouble their efforts to be as engaged as possible in the external world. So much depends on personality. Yet to pursue a more contemplative way of aging involves some "doing," even though much of it is of a more interior sort. And, of course, it involves a far different mode of being than would be posited by the activity theory of aging. Walt Whitman caught the sense of this difference when he quipped, in the spirit of Lao Tzu, "The way to do is to be." Being comes first, but what is *that* like and how is it experienced?

The intention of contemplation is not willful mastery but, rather, opening the mind and beholding. This involves a shift in mind and body. Thinking is for action, control, acquisition. It is a conscious, effortful activity that is clearly in the doing mode. Contemplation requires a receptive, being mode, which attends to what emerges in consciousness without willfulness or direction. The neuro-physiological features of the active doing state include a tensing of the large muscles, a narrow focusing of the eyes, and lessening of sensual awareness, while the neurological activity of the brain occurs in fast and short electrical currents. But in the more receptive mode of contemplation, the muscles relax, vision softens, the senses unfold, and the brain waves become slow, somewhat irregular, and higher (i.e., more alpha waves), indicating an attitudinal change. This mode is essentially one of relaxing and beholding, whereas the action mode is one of tensing and directing consciousness toward doing something. With conscious doing we divide and conquer our environment; with the receptive mode we take in, merge, unify. It is not activity versus passivity, for beholding is an activity that falls more into the being mode. It has been said that the beginnings of philosophy are slow because wisdom does not inspect but beholds, and we must look patiently before we can see beyond appearances.

The beginning of this wisdom involves a deliberate slowing down and becoming mindful of everything one sees, hears, and senses. For younger persons this has to be deliberate, because of their high natural energy level, while for the elderly it is more part of a natural process. The inevitable physical slowing down and development of interiority can lead to a new perspective on one's self and existence, and also lead to a new, unveiled reality. One nursing-home resident expressed this change to me, as follows:

> I've been told that I must not succumb to the facts of my age. But why shouldn't I? I am now in my ninety-first year, and I doubt that my activity, for example in civic affairs, could restore my spirits to a state of bouncing buoyancy. Lack of physical strength alone keeps me inactive and often silent. I've been called senile. Senility is a convenient peg on which to hang nonconformity. A new set of faculties seems to be coming into operation. I seem to be awakening to a larger world of wonderment, to catch little glimpses of the immensity and diversity of creation. More than at any other time in my life, I seem to be aware of the beauties of our spinning planet and the sky above. I feel that old age sharpens my awareness.

This woman has described eloquently a phenomenon of old age, the cosmic consciousness of gerotranscendence.

The Question of Transcendence

As noted in the Introduction, the theory of gerotranscendence was developed and described by Lars Tornstam (2005), a gerontologist at the University of Uppsala in Sweden. He and his colleagues, based on their surveys of Scandinavian populations, described the phenomenon of gerotranscendence as a shift in metaperspective from a rational and materialistic view of the world and reality to a more transcendent one. This is often accompanied by a new understanding of existence itself, which involves a redefinition of time, space, life, and death. The elder attempts to integrate the experience of union with the universe into a more mystical world view, in which there is less interest in the egoistic self and its more youthful social agendas.

My research and that of other gerontologists suggest that certain of Tornstams's interpretations hold up for most older Americans, but some of his ideas need to be reconsidered or reconfigured on the basis of subsequent empirical findings. Nevertheless, the key element in Tornstam's description of gerotranscendence is the shift in metaperspective with the advent of old age. To understand this shift, one needs to look at it from a neurological and developmental point of view. The human brain and nervous system have been likened to a complex stimulus-reduction system, which protects us from being thoroughly confused and overwhelmed by the mass of largely random and purposeless stimuli and data assailing us at each and every moment. The reducing function of this system enables us to perceive only a very small and particular selection of those stimuli and data—those that are apt to be practical and useful in our basic concern with physical and social survival. So the larger perspective of "Mind at Large" has to be funneled through this reducing valve, to leave us with the narrower kind of consciousness that will allow us to survive on this particular planet at this particular place and time in human history. Society and culture further enable this funneling process. A great deal of this reduction is accomplished through the medium of language, so most people ordinarily only know or accept that which is consecrated as genuinely real by the local language. Each belief or language system imposes its own reductive kind of knowledge of "reality" onto the formless flux of sensations and stimuli. This is done cognitively by naming and categorizing the elements of this flux through language. One eminent linguist (Whorf, 1956) stated that the result of imposing such categories is an artificial chopping up of the continuous spread and flow of human experience. When we get old and are physically made to slow down, we have the opportunity to see and appreciate more of the myriad objects and phenomena in our immediate experience and daily existence. For example, when we are at the beach we may notice the individual grains of sand and wonder about the eons of history represented in one grain, shaped by the many waves and intersecting clashes of wind over the centuries, rather than only focusing on whether the sand is too hot or too wet to feel entirely comfortable at the moment. Thus, more of the particularities in the immensity of our world become available to us in later life. This represents a shift of perspective that provides for a sense of immanent spirituality, in addition to the transcendence of cosmic consciousness in later life.

One of the most influential experts in the psychology of aging (Peck, 1968) proposed three major areas requiring transcendence in the latter years of life: (1) ego differentiation versus work-role preoccupation, (2) body transcendence versus body preoccupation, and (3) ego transcendence versus ego preoccupation. The first area concerns the impact of retirement and loss of major social and economic roles on the individual's sense of self. The more one's ego identity and self-esteem are bound up in societal roles, the greater is the work-role preoccupation, and the less is one's sense of self-worth, when the work role has ended. Ego differentiation refers to the development of alternative interests from one's occupational role and status, which allow for a continued sense of self-worth and life satisfaction; and to the development of different ways of thinking and being, which can transcend the loss of work roles, as well as the lessening of physical capacities and attractiveness.

For those who have placed primary value on physical health, activity, and attractiveness, physical decline represents a grave insult to their sense of self and well-being. The result is often a pervasive preoccupation with their bodies—the aches, pains, blemishes, and so on. Getting beyond this preoccupation requires a shift toward a more philosophical or spiritual approach to bodily change.

The third area of ego transcendence versus ego preoccupation is concerned with the certain prospect of one's death and the extinction of the ego. When one cannot come to terms with this outlook, there is a narcissistic self-concern, anxiety, and fear of death. Acceptance of one's own mortality is obviously a prerequisite for ego transcendence. Some degree of ego transcendence can also be achieved by living generously and unselfishly, so as to leave contributions to the culture that will last beyond one's personal death, through children, grandchildren, friendships, and charitable service or contributions. In later life, however, if one can no longer live generously because of loss of physical capacities and financial resources, then there *has* to be another way to achieve such transcendence. There needs to be an alternative to the narcissistic self-concern, anxiety, and preoccupation with death and the meaninglessness that is despair.

There is an alternative way that allows for the sense of being part of the whole of life, not just the cycle of birth and death, of something larger than one's self, in which one identifies with the cosmic and the eternal, thereby transcending one's limited, mortal perspective. But the manner in which it comes about is not by trying *symbolically* to project one's self to an elevated transcendent state of union with the cosmos. Experientially it is much more sensate and inwardly grounded, even though the body is weakened and made less vital by age. This truth was recognized and even described in the New Testament, 2 Corinthians (4:16) with these words: "Though our outer nature is wasting away, our inner nature is being renewed every day."

Robert Butler (1970), the noted gero-psychiatrist, has referred to this way of transcendence as "indwelling." He used this term in an informal discussion, and based it on both his long professional practice with the elderly and personal experience, as he approached age 80. According to his description, it builds on the natural interiority of old age, and involves attending to something inside of yourself that does not feel that it is changing or aging at all. It is a consciousness that recognizes one's body is aging, as are the people and things around you. Yet you know, within this consciousness, that something about you is not aging at all, as Butler indicated in his quote from Tolstoy (presented in Chapter Three).

Descartes claimed that there is a self, simple and abiding throughout our changing experiences. William James wrote that common sense would drive us to admit such a self. He felt it was a self outside physical changes, one that is permanent and opposed to the "changing and inconstant," but one felt by all men. This self has been called the "transcendental ego" in various philosophies, and the "pure ego," Atman, or Ruh in some religious traditions. The late Princeton professor of philosophy Walter Stace (1961) called this type of transcendence an "introvertive," mystical type of experience, which he claimed was the same throughout the world, in every culture, religion, place, and age.

David Gutmann (1964), on the basis of his stage theory of old age, would probably say this is an example of what he called "magical" mastery (*omniplasty*) rather than "mystical" experience. But it should be noted that he was writing from a much narrower frame of reference as an ego-psychologist. From that theoretical perspective, he would see such a transcendent or mystical mind set as defensive and regressive, because it is far removed from the ego's drive to master or control the outer and inner world. Whether it is a magical or mystical experiential state of consciousness is probably more than a semantic question, and probably depends on the individual experiencing it. If the older individual has achieved the psychological maturity called ego integrity, then the experiential state is probably mystical, transcendent, and emotionally healthy rather than magical, defensive, and regressive.

Erich Fromm (1992), as a classically trained yet post-Freudian psychoanalyst, was well versed in ego psychology; but he also saw the development of mysticism as a natural outcome of the evolution of humans as psycho-social beings. Mystical consciousness is not magical or fantastic in any superstitious or regressive sense. He reasoned that at a certain point of human development, when we humans had severed most of the primal ties that made us part of the soil and our own tribe, we became more individuated and aware of ourselves as individual beings faced with an immense variety of stimuli and challenges from our environment and others. Therefore, humans had to develop the capacity to distinguish the world of the many, the phenomenal world, and the alternative view of the world, i.e., the world of the One, or the *No-thing*, so as not to be overwhelmed by the multitude of attractions and repulsions in the phenomenal world. Therefore, we humans have had to build the idea of the One in ourselves as a regulating principle of cognition and self-experience, so as not to become the helpless object of myriad things and our reflexive reactions to them. We had to begin to experience ourselves as subjects in a multitudinous object world.

Fromm goes on to note that the principal of the One was established as far back as the very early Upanishads in ancient India, in which Brahman was seen as the principal of the One in the universe, which is identical with the principal of the One in the person, the Atman. The One transcends all that exists and is not somebody or something; it is *neti, neti*, meaning it is not this or that. In Buddhism, as well, the "highest" is absolute "voidness," or emptiness, which cannot be known but only hinted at by what it is *not*. In more modern times, Sartre (1966) referred to this voidness or emptiness as a person's intuition of nothingness.

Ancient Chinese Taoism was founded on the idea that the One, or the Tao, could not be described in language. Words are just signs to point to the nonconceptual ultimate reality. As it says in the *Tao Te Ching*, "The Tao that can be spoken of is not the real Tao. The name that can be named is not the true name." Fromm points out that Zen Buddhism, which was much influenced by Taoism, also claims that the One can neither be expressed in language nor understood through discursive means. Further, the same claim was made in Western philosophy and mysticism by the likes of Plotinus, Boethius, Eckhart, and Pseudo-Dionysius the Areopagite.

This ancient concept of the inexpressible One was, in a sense, coopted by the monotheistic concept of God, which began to be expressed in anthropomorphic language as the "King" or "King of Kings." Soon this idolization of God began to dominate the thinking of the masses and their leaders, and developed into a widespread and popular orthodoxy. However, there were those in both Judaism and Christianity who attempted to restore the original pure concept of the One and to resist the process of idolization. The "negative theology" of Maimonides held that one can say what God is *not*, but there can be no positive assertion about what God *is*. This negative theology comes out of the biblical tradition that prohibited the representation or worship of God by images, statues, or other symbolic props. Yet without these props a negative theology will cleanse the place where man, approaching the thought of God by way of a *not*, can nevertheless, paradoxically, experience the divine reality. Thus, negative theology becomes the way of not knowing, the *via negativa*, toward the divine. It is a mystical way but there are discernable articles of faith within it throughout the various traditions in which it is found. These articles include the willingness to surrender to the natural flow of the world; to recognize the futility of pursuing material gains and satisfactions as worthy goals; to recognize the possibility of reaching a mode of existence that is superior to our usual one; and to feel the unknowable presence or force that is no-thing, that can only be defined by negatives, because it is not part of the object world yet is immanent in every person and everything.

This is also known as *apophatic* mysticism. In order to experience a sense of union, or oneness, the apophatic mystic suspends all beliefs and disbeliefs, and with an empty mind enters into a state of surrender and pure being, without thought or emotion. Apophatic theology is based on the *via negativa,* which has been called the way of God through negation, prevalent in both Eastern and Western mysticism. No predicates attach to God; no words may legitimately be used to describe God. He is "not this, not that;" so by stripping from our imaginings and illusions about God, and eliminating all that is not God, we begin to penetrate to the heart of the mystery. The converse of the *via negativa* is the *via affirmativa*, which is the way of affirmation by approaching God through positive assertion about His attributes. He is defined as good, just, wise, loving, and so on, expanding our concept from goodness as we know it to infinite goodness. He is also invariably a "He." Many theologians claim that the *via affirmativa* is inadequate without the *via negativa*, because it, can speak only of the attributes of God, never of His eternal nature.

In all traditions there is a way of viewing spirituality that emphasizes the importance of images, symbols, and sensations. This kind of spirituality, classically known as *kataphatic,* has always been more popular and seeks deeper realization of God through visions, feelings, imagery, words, and other sensate or symbolic forms of experience. The apophatic way seeks the truth of God that lies behind, beyond, or hidden within all sensory or intellectual representations. The kataphatic way is characteristic of evangelical and charismatic Christianity, popular Hinduism, and even Tantric Buddhism. The apophatic way has been found in the Christian mysticism of John of the Cross, Meister Eckhart, *The Cloud of Unknowing*, and the silence of Quaker meetings. The emptiness or no-mind of Zen Buddhism would also be a distinctly apophatic spirituality. In nearly all traditions we find elements of both apophatic and kataphatic approaches, but one or the other is usually dominant. In most cases the kataphatic way will predominate. However, it should be noted that most people who end up with an apophatic orientation have gone through a number of kataphatic phases and experiences along their way (Stace, 1960).

Younger people and individuals just beginning the process of intentional spiritual seeking almost invariably start off with a kataphatic orientation, in which they seek substantial experience and a sense of assurance of their relationship with the divine. Their expectation is that this occurs through the senses, imagery, and thought. Some people will continue to seek out such sensory experience for years before developing any deep attraction to the mystery behind and beyond sensate experience. Negative theology means opening to the mystery of the divine presence within us that transcends the capacity of every human faculty, and even the theological differences between East and West. In the West we have had apophatic thinkers through the centuries, such as Eckhart and Kierkegaard, and the same has been true in the East. D.T. Suzuki (1979), a Zen Buddhist and philosopher, notes the closeness of Meister Eckhart's mysticism to Taoism and Mahayana Buddhism, particularly concerning the concept of being. He quotes Eckhart as follows: "Being is God . . . God and being are the same" (Suzuki, 1979, p. 4).

Suzuki makes an interesting observation about the psychological dimension regarding kataphatic and apophatic faith. He notes that there are always two opposing tendencies in the human way of thinking and feeling: extravert and introvert, outer and inner, objective and subjective, exoteric and esoteric, traditional and mystical. Often the opposition between these polar tendencies or temperaments is too deep and strong for any form of reconciliation, which is why orthodox and traditional Christians of Eckhart's time considered him a heretic. Kierkegaard, an apophatic, was also considered a heretic by orthodox Christians in nineteenth century Denmark. He claimed it was not by the exoteric or objective viewpoint that questions of faith could be meaningfully raised, but only by the subjective, inner viewpoint. Here again, perhaps, introverts are apt to find that apophatic faith comes to them more naturally than to extraverts, much as contemplative aging does. It should also be noted that apophatic faith would seem to be more acceptable to an agnostic, given the definition of an agnostic as a person who holds the view that any ultimate reality (such as God) is unknown and probably unknowable. What would an apophatic faith, with its emphasis on being rather than doing, consist of and what would be its aims? This will be explored in the following section.

The Mystical Dimension

Einstein, the ultimate scientist, once made an interesting observation: "The most profound and sublime experience of which man is capable is the awareness of the mystical." In the later stages of life, if the older person grows into the philosophical style Erikson described, it is not uncommon for a mystical element to develop in his or her consciousness. I can recall one elder with a philosophical education and background commenting that the study of metaphysics is the necessary ripening process to prepare one for mysticism. Chuang Tzu held that mystical philosophy is for the nourishment of the individual, and particularly so for the aged individual. Whether this is the usual ripening process I do not know, but among many elders, according to Tornstam's theory of gerotranscendence, mysticism often takes the form of an intuition of the union of the finite self with the universe. Another prominent gerontologist, Robert Atchley (1997), claims that the contemplative, mystical experience is at the heart of spiritual development in later adulthood. He refers to it as "everyday mysticism" and notes that the reduced social demands of later life combine to facilitate mystical experience as part of everyday life. Ironically, by excluding elders from the mainstream, societies may actually create social conditions that foster their spiritual growth.

It is important, however, to distinguish rare mystical events of illumination and revelation from what Atchley refers to as the everyday mysticism of later adulthood, or what is referred to here as the mystical dimension. When Tornstam refers to the cosmic dimension or cosmic consciousness in his theory of gerotranscendence, it should be recognized that he is not referring to those ecstatic mystical events. Richard Bucke (1923), in his classic *Cosmic Consciousness*, was referring to extraordinary events. His own first experience with such an ecstatic event occurred on a ride home in the late evening after he and two friends had spent the evening reading and discussing the poetry of Wordsworth, Shelley, Keats, and, especially, Whitman. He described the event in the third person and claimed that he was in a state of quiet, almost passive, enjoyment when suddenly he found himself wrapped in a flame-colored cloud that he thought was a conflagration in the local city. Yet in the next instant he knew that the light was "within himself," and he had a sense of exultation and immense joyousness, accompanied by an intellectual illumination he found impossible to describe. This was certainly an ecstatic experience. It has all four of the characteristics that William James (1961) claimed to be common to all such mystical experiences. These characteristics are ineffability, noetic quality, transiency, and passivity. In Bucke's words, the experience was "quite impossible to describe," hence ineffable. It was an "*intellectual* illumination," hence noetic, as well as an emotional one. Of course, the experience was transient, for such out-of-self events cannot last if we are to function in our normal everyday world. Finally, it was not actively sought, but passive, occurring "in a state of quiet," when it happened.

Although the everyday mysticism of later life does not include all four of these characteristics simultaneously, it does partake of some of them some of the time. There is invariably a certain turning inward and a stillness of the mind. Frequently there is also a deep peacefulness, joy, and utter absorption in the immediate situation, and this sometimes feels as though one is making contact with an ultimate reality. On rare occasions there might even be an illuminating noetic experience, in which one *knows* directly that there is a reality completely unknown in one's previous experience.

A somewhat different kind of mystical experience occurred to William James (1961), when he was experimenting with nitrous oxide to see if a similar depth of revelatory truth would manifest itself to him. Indeed, as he commented, "the keynote of the experience is the tremendously exciting sense of an intense metaphysical illumination." At its acme the nitrous oxide mystical experience was characterized by an "immense emotional sense of *reconciliation,*" in which "the centre and periphery of things seem to come together" [and]

> every opposition . . . vanishes in a higher unity in which it is based; that all contradictions, so called, are but differences; that all differences are of degree; that all degrees are of a common kind; that unbroken continuity is the essence of being. . . . It is impossible to convey an idea of the torrential character of the identification of opposites as it streams through the mind in this experience. . . . God and devil, good and evil, life and death, I and thou, sober and drunk, matter and form, black and white, quantity and quality . . . and fifty other contrasts. . . . were manifested in this experience. (1961, p. 295)

Note that this was not a total "cosmic" event in which James felt at one with the universe and, further, it was induced by the nitrous oxide. Nevertheless, it was at a level that transcended the dualities of human existence to a point where it could be called truly encompassing. It was undoubtedly noetic in the sense that there was a feeling of utter certainty about the truth of what he was experiencing. Having had the same kind of experience (although not under the influence of nitrous oxide), an epiphany of the encompassing reconciliation of opposites, I can personally attest to a feeling of unequivocal certainty about the ultimate reconciliation of opposites. Of course James believed that the psyche is a nexus of constantly changing and interrelated fields that are integrally linked with wider and deeper levels of consciousness. These levels of consciousness are what flood into ordinary awareness during mystical experiences. The widest possible field of consciousness can be seen as both separate and connected, which provides James with a philosophical position in which the further limits of our being can be seen as merging into a "mother-sea" of consciousness without violating our integrity and individuality. So these epiphanies or states of mystical intuition can be seen as very sudden and immense extensions of the ordinary field of consciousness. James proposed that the way to look at it is to imagine it as a wave in an ocean that, while momentarily rising above sea level, also remains in its depths connected with the ocean and with all the other waves of awareness.

According to James, such mystical experiences cannot be forced or willed. They arise on their own. Meditation, prayer, and other practices might prepare the way for them but they do not guarantee them. Also these immediate and intuitive apprehensions of a spiritual dimension cannot be captured by language, no matter how expressive; but they have to be experienced within oneself, for there is a quality or feeling which is affective and not cognitive. He felt that by returning to a simpler and more elemental existence life can become intensely interesting at the non-thinking level, the level of "pure sensorial perception." This is much in line with the everyday mysticism of later life described by Atchley (1997), i.e., the development of a capacity to look deeply into the ordinary.

Other philosophers besides James have attempted to identify the common features of mystical experience across cultures and spiritual traditions. One of the more widely known is the conception of Walter Stace (1961), mentioned earlier. As a philosopher, he was careful about what should and should not be included in any definition of the term "mysticism." He held that visions, voices, or powerful dreams are not mystical experiences. The singular feature of a mystical experience is the apprehension of an ultimately non-sensuous unity in all things, a oneness or a One that neither the senses nor the reason can penetrate. By the word "mystic" he specifically means a person who actually has such mystical experiences. He adds that the word "mysticism" is often mistakenly used in the sense of misty, foggy, or vague, and is emphatic in stating there is nothing misty, foggy, or vague about mysticism. It is also not the same as the "occult," nor does it include parapsychological phenomena like telepathy, clairvoyance, telekinesis, or precognition.

Stace claimed that there are two types of mystical experience. One is called *extravertive* and the other *introvertive*. The extravertive way looks outward through the physical senses into the external world to apprehend the One or the Oneness of all through the multiplicity of the world. The Oneness is experienced as a sacred objective reality in ings of bliss and joy. The introvertive way turns inward, and introspec tively finds the One at the most inward core of the self or soul. It is more monastic and figures more prominently in the history of mysticism, East and West. The extravertive mystic senses the same world of trees, chairs, tables, and things in general as the rest of us, but sees these objects transfigured in such a way that the Unity of the One shines through them. It has been said that the great Chinese landscape paintings of the Song dynasty onwards expressed the sense of a mystical union of the individual human with the natural world, and were referred to as "mysticism made visible." Stace suggests that the extravertive experience is a kind of halfway house to the introvertive, because it includes ordinary sense perceptions and, in that respect, it is kataphatic. The introvertive is wholly nonsensuous and nonintellectual. It is beyond the senses, beyond the understanding, beyond all expression in a pure unitary consciousness without any sensate or intellectual content. Stace claims the introvertive experience is the same across cultures and only the interpretations of the experience differ. For example, theistic mystics are apt to interpret the experience theistically because of their theology, whereas the nontheistic Buddhists would have no such interpretations.

Stace was something of a purist in stating that only experiences that involve the apprehension of an ultimate nonsensuous unity in all things, which the senses and reason cannot penetrate, are truly mystical. There are experiences that lack this central feature but, nevertheless, possess other mystical characteristics. These could be called borderline cases, which tend to shade off from the central core cases. Not all philosophers would hue entirely to Stace's definitions. William James (1961), for example, claimed that the varieties of religious and mystical experiences are dependent on the varieties of human nature. On this basis, it would be safe to say that introverts would find it less difficult to enter this mystic dimension of later life, since they more naturally take to interiority and introspection. Extraverts, on the other hand, would tend to be stimulated by external things *per se* and, perhaps, have difficulty quieting their senses and intellect to see beneath them in some transformative sense. On the other hand, they can have mystical experiences of the extravertive and kataphatic type.

ng of the everyday mysticism of later life, Atchley a compelling definition of mysticism, i.e., *the direct ex- ground of all being*. However, even if the elder does not prehension of the ground of all being, there is apt to be a sence and reality. This is, in all likelihood, the "cosmic consciousness" to which Tornstam refers in his theory of gerotranscendence. The key to the mystical element lies in *intuition,* with its roots in the Latin term *intueri*, which means to look at and to contemplate.

Contemplative Happiness

Socrates and Aristotle both defined the best life as the contemplative life. For Aristotle, this was based on the notion of *eudemonia*, or human flourishing. *Eudamonia* is usually translated as happiness or well-being, but there are several different versions, even among the ancient Greeks, of what it is to truly flourish. One variation defines *eudamonia* as the condition of living in harmony with one's *daimon*, or innate potentiality. This is essentially the same idea as James Hillman (1996) puts forth, which is that character is destiny and one should live in truth to oneself. Thus, in a contemplative old age, the force of character should come through and one should come to live more truly as oneself. Aristotle himself displayed some variations in his thinking about *eudamonia.* For example, he saw it as related to "success," since living well means doing well, and this usually goes hand-in-hand with the *active* life. Yet, this seems at odds with the fact that he extolled the life of study as the essential realization of *eudamonia.* We don't usually equate the active life with a life of study. Ultimately, though, Aristotle seemed to come to the conclusion that *eudamonia* is the doing of that which is done for its own sake, as the gods did. He came to believe that contemplation itself was the ultimate *telos* and state of mind that provides the greatest happiness in its own right.

It is this conception of *eudamonia* as happiness that seems to have the greatest implications for a contemplative old age. This conception was developed to the fullest extent by Thomas Aquinas, who came to the conclusion that contemplation *is* happiness. Of course, Aquinas saw this from a theological point of view, as the eternal contemplation of God, but it can also be seen as contemplation of the good or the One, as Plotinus saw it. The key point for a contemplative later life lies in the idea of contemplation as doing that which is done for its own sake. This is contemplative happiness or contemplation *as* happiness. It is this idea that finally led Aristotle to claim that "Happiness is the best, noblest, and most pleasant thing in the world." The same idea led St. Augustine to observe that "Man has no reason to philosophize except with a view to happiness," and Plato to say that "The utmost happiness takes the form of contemplation." But behind these observations is the idea that contemplation, whether it be called philosophizing or simply beholding with an open mind, is something that is done for its own sake.

Thus, contemplation is similar to play, something that is done largely for the sheer pleasure of it, without any end or purpose involved. Philo, the ancient Jewish philosopher who achieved a far-reaching synthesis between Greek and Jewish thought, claimed that the goal of wisdom is laughter and play—not the kind that one sees in small children who do not yet have the faculty of reason, but the kind that is developed in those who have grown mature through both time and understanding. For if someone has experienced the wisdom that can only be heard from oneself, learned from oneself, and created from oneself, then he or she does not merely participate in laughter but becomes laughter itself.

Perhaps more than any other recent thinker, the German philosopher Joseph Pieper pursued this idea of contemplation as happiness. In his book *Happiness and Contemplation* (1958), he states flatly that "man's ultimate happiness consists in contemplation," and goes on to say that this statement "contains a whole philosophy of life, a basic conception of man and the meaning of human existence" (p. 92). According to Pieper, the whole energy of our being is ultimately directed toward attainment of insight, and this kind of "seeing-into" is best done in contemplation. It is a form of knowing arrived at not by thinking but by inner sight, by intuition; and the ultimate intuition is to see that all things are "good," despite appearances, and beyond all explanation. Seeing this, one is happy. Contemplation of the divine good underlying all things is not a matter of morality, for Pieper claims that we must recognize that the whole of morality points to something beyond itself; that it makes arrangements for something else; that, in any case, its purpose does not simply lie within itself, and that it therefore cannot constitute the ultimate purpose of life. It can, however, enter into the ultimate purpose, that purpose being happiness.

Chapter Five

Contemplative Practice

We generally think of contemplation as being a careful consideration or study of weighty matters or ideas, or as a sustained, intense viewing of an object or phenomenon that has captured our attention, which we want to explore further. This is not far from most dictionary definitions of contemplation, one of which is "The act of mind in considering with attention; meditation; study; consideration; the act of thinking about something intently." Contemplation is also thought of as meditation, which has the additional meanings of a state of "relaxed concentration on the reality of the present moment;" a state that "is experienced when the mind is free of all thoughts;" a state of "concentrated attention, liberated from restlessness," and also a state of "deep continued thought . . . and . . . solemn reflection on sacred matters."

These definitions indicate that there are various forms of contemplation that involve different acts, such as thinking, observing and attending, studying, meditating, and praying. Given the immense range of contemplative practices in the various traditions and cultures of the world, it is best for us to focus primarily on those practices and methods that pertain to a contemplative old age. Such practices should take into account the physical and psychological developments of later life that have been described in the previous chapters of this book. In particular, they should take into account the temporal limitation inherent in the last developmental stage of life. Younger persons can go to India or Tibet and study with a guru or undertake lengthy and intensive training in America, among other possible options. Elders, however, as beginners, do not have the luxury of a lifetime ahead of them for such training and meditative refinement.

Meditation and the Art of Being

Since the primary concern of this book is contemplation as a way of being in later life, we would do well, at this point, to go back to the experience of Erich Fromm (1992), who in his remaining years chose a contemplative practice, which he described in *The Art of Being.* He stated that a basic preparation for learning the art of being is to meditate, and the best form of meditation for this purpose is the mindfulness type, in which breath is the focal point. Breath is a well-chosen vehicle for meditative practice because of its centrality to life and existence, to being. It is the bridge that connects life to consciousness and unites body to thoughts; and breath has strong spiritual connotations across cultures, as evidenced by the fact that the words for spirit and breath are often synonymous in various cultures, e.g., Greek (*pneuma*), Latin (*spiritus*), Hebrew (*ruach*), and Sanskrit (*prana*). In Christianity, *soma* (body) has been seen as the psycho-physical unity that was made in the image of God and, when permeated with the breath (*pneuma*), represents the Spirit of God. Of course, breath is a sign of *being* (alive) in a literal sense. So in meditative practice one often gets the feeling that breathing and being are one and the same thing, and that, together, they provide a unitive experience that is spiritual in nature.

Although attending to the breath is central in sitting meditation, mindfulness can be applied in as many of our daily activities of living as possible. This means giving full attention to activities such as walking, eating, thinking, hearing, and seeing. Any of the myriad chores that ordinarily bore us and that we usually do in a routine, unmindful way, if done with mindfulness, become more manifest, distinct, and valued in their simple reality. Thus, living becomes fully transparent through full awareness. Each activity, such as washing dishes, peeling potatoes, hoeing the garden can be done as a sort of rite, with mindfulness and reverence, to allow one to experience the preciousness and sanctity each moment of living can have. It helps us appreciate what is often called "the holiness of everyday life."

The beginning instructions for sitting mindfulness meditation are easy and direct. First, one finds a quiet comfortable place to sit alone without distraction or interruption. It is not necessary for elders to sit cross-legged on a mat in the lotus position; they can use a chair and cushions for comfort. However, one's back should be kept straight and the body firmly seated, but relaxed, with the eyes lightly closed. The next step is to gently let go of any physical tension one might be feeling. The focus of attention in this meditation is consistently on the breath, noticing the place where it is felt most clearly (in the nose, the chest, or the abdomen), and simply observing its flow—in and out, rising and falling. The mind will undoubtedly wander; thoughts will come and go in a sort of mental chatter. Distractions, questions, and doubts will arise, but whenever they do, you simply remember to bring attention back to the breath. Practice begins by sitting for just 10 or 20 minutes, and can be increased or varied over time. The ending should feel natural, unforced, and refreshing.

As one comes back to the breath, time and again, mindfulness tends to grow stronger and more stable. Then it is possible to leave the breath for a while and simply notice whatever arises in consciousness through hearing, seeing, sensing, feeling, or thinking. Thus, there is a sense of *allowing*, and simply being with whatever presents itself: an emotion, a physical discomfort, a thought, anything. The first core guideline for mindfulness meditation is to be mindfully aware of whatever presents itself. The second step is to notice how one relates to whatever arises. Our usual way of relating is reactive: if we like it, we try to hold on to it; if we don't like it, we pull back out of fear or aversion. Instead, one should simply allow space for whatever is going on, simply observe it rather than identify with it, and stop trying to make things different. A helpful phrase to work with is "Let it be," recognizing that everything comes and goes by itself, that nothing has to be done to make it come, or to make it go. We just let it be. The key point, then, is not whether we experience pleasant or unpleasant feelings, but how we *relate* to those feelings. The mindful way is to simply observe them in passing, and in that moment we become free from a greedy desire for the pleasant feelings or a strong aversion to the unpleasant. Such practice facilitates a transcendence of both the body and ego preoccupations that plague many elders. The relaxed gentleness of the conditions and instructions of the practice are well suited for their stage of life. While some people consider meditation an evasion of reality, it is in fact a serene and grateful encounter with it.

A common experience in beginning mindfulness meditation is a sense of aimlessness. This is not necessarily a problem, however, since meditation is intended to be a pleasure in itself, though many of us feel lost without a sense of structure or direction. One of the foremost teachers of mindfulness is Thich Nhat Hanh, a Vietnamese Buddhist monk. He is also a scholar and a peace activist who was nominated for the Nobel Peace Prize by Martin Luther King. One of his highly instructive books deals with the sense of aimlessness, by providing a progression of

steps in the meditative process called the "*sutra* on th
breathing" (Hanh, 1996). English translation of this
cient Pali and Sanskrit texts, and consists of sixte
and exhaling in what are called the Four Establishm
Everything that exists can be placed in one of the Four, wh
body, (2) the feelings, (3) the mind, and (4) the objects of the mi
sixteen methods, which are given below, will be elaborated later in terms of the philosophy and the theory that underlies the practice, i.e., mindfulness as praxis. It should be noted that the meaning of the word *dharmas*, as used in these steps, simply means things or forms of all sorts.

When one is comfortably seated and the eyes are lightly closed, a preparatory step is to feel and to say silently to oneself, "Breathing in I'm aware I am breathing in. Breathing out I'm aware I am breathing out." Then one proceeds sequentially with the following steps:

1. Breathing in a long breath I'm aware I am breathing in a long breath. Breathing out a long breath I'm aware I am breathing out a long breath.
2. Breathing in a short breath I'm aware I am breathing in a short breath. Breathing out a short breath I'm aware I am breathing out a short breath.
3. Breathing in I am aware of my whole body. Breathing out I am aware of my whole body.
4. Breathing in I calm my whole body. Breathing out I calm my whole body.
5. Breathing in I can feel joyful. Breathing out I can feel joyful.
6. Breathing in I can feel happy. Breathing out I can feel happy.
7. Breathing in I am aware of my mental formations. Breathing out I am aware of my mental formations.
8. Breathing in I calm my mental formations. Breathing out I calm my mental formations.
9. Breathing in I am aware of my mind. Breathing out I am aware of my mind.
10. Breathing in I make my mind happy. Breathing out I make my mind happy.
11. Breathing in I concentrate my mind. Breathing out I concentrate my mind.

mi

2. Breathing in I liberate my mind. Breathing out I liberate my .d.

13. Breathing in I observe the impermanent nature of all *dharmas*. Breathing out I observe the impermanent nature of all *dharmas*.

14. Breathing in I observe the disappearance of desire. Breathing out I observe the disappearance of desire.

15. Breathing in I observe cessation. Breathing out I observe cessation.

16. Breathing in I observe letting go. Breathing out I observe letting go. (Hanh, 1996, pp. 23-27)

The first four exercises help to establish mindfulness of the body, to create harmony and ease in reuniting body and mind. In the first two steps, the object of awareness is the breath itself, such that our mind is the subject and our breathing is the object; and we recognize that our breathing affects our mind, and our mind affects our breathing. The third and fourth steps call attention to the whole body, not just the breathing function, and help to calm the whole body and the mind with it.

The next four exercises concern our feelings and are intended to elicit feelings of joy and happiness so as to transform emotional suffering. The fifth step concerning joy aims at developing a positive psychological and physiological state. In the process we are apt to touch on unpleasant as well as pleasant and neutral feelings. The unpleasant should be recognized and allowed to cross our minds without avoidance, only to return ourselves to a more pleasant state of mind. The sixth step involving happiness is more than joy in Buddhist thinking. Joy is considered less pure because there can be excitement in it. In the beginning we need joy, but as we develop happiness the excitement present in joy disappears, and a more modulated and enduring sense of well being permeates our consciousness. Happiness in itself is considered nourishing, and as it is strengthened through mindfulness meditation we do not have to look outside ourselves in order to have it. This underlines the fact that meditation is a way of *being*, not just a technique.

The seventh and eighth exercises on mental formations are also about feelings, but more than eliciting feelings like joy and happiness, the purpose is to be aware of the feeling that is present right now. All feelings, pleasant and unpleasant, are to be observed. So feelings of irritation, anger, anxiety, and weariness are recognized and observed. This idea of "looking deeply" is based on non-duality and is designed so that we do not view these feelings as outside coming in but, simply, as part of this moment of awareness. By looking deeply, no barriers are set up between good and bad in ourselves, which can make our minds into moral battlefields. By observing the feeling we can see how it arises, stays for a while, and then ceases to be. This helps us view our thoughts and feelings as phenomena that come and go.

Since all consciousness is consciousness of something, we become aware of our mind in the ninth exercise by being aware of its object, the breath. It is as though our mind and our breath become one in the process. This then leads naturally into the tenth exercise in which we silently say, "Breathing in, I make my mind happy, Breathing out, I make my mind happy." This is intended to elicit the positive mental formations that are already within us, and to have confidence and faith that the path we are following is a beneficial one. Next, the eleventh exercise is to concentrate our mind on the formation that is manifesting itself at that moment, such as faith and confidence. Then, when we say "liberate my mind" in the twelfth exercise, we are freeing the mind from any mental formation that makes us anxious, confused, or pushes us in the wrong direction.

The thirteenth exercise is intended to observe and recognize the impermanent nature of all *dharmas*. Recall that in this context *dharmas* simply mean formations, things or phenomena. So all phenomena, whether material, psychological, or physiological, are seen as impermanent and transient without exception. Some things seem more permanent than others, but if looked at deeply they will be recognized as much slower processes of change. Modern, sub-atomic science has certainly demonstrated this for us. Getting rid of intense, grasping desire for things, success, love, respect and so on is the purpose of the fourteenth exercise. If we see that the nature of the object of our desire is always changing and on the way to dissolution, our intense desire not to lose it will also disappear. If we can extend our narrow view of a concretely existing self we can see that our life consists in everything, the all or the One. This then flows naturally into the fifteenth exercise in which, by breathing in and out, we observe cessation of illusion, of *Maya* or all those notions that keep us from experiencing actual reality. This means cessation of categorical thinking, as in ideas of permanence and annihilation, birth and death, coming and going. They are simply seen as inseparable aspects of a larger reality rather than as permanently opposed entities.

With the sixteenth exercise, we observe letting go in the sense of giving up intense desire and attachment, fear and anxiety, hatred and anger, all the erroneous ideas that cause us suffering. This particular exercise can be greatly enhanced if the words "letting" and "go" are attuned directly to the breath, thus the word "letting" can accompany the natural arising of the in-breath and the word "go" accompanies the natural release of the out-breath. This can be repeated several times, and it provides a truly unified and embodied sense of letting go.

It is not necessary to practice all sixteen exercises in one sitting. One or more exercises can be practiced as long as ten minutes each, whatever feels right at the time. As long as the practice is enjoyable and we are nourished by it, we are practicing correctly. It is also fine to add different exercises that enhance your practice and your path or faith. For example, I find it helpful and reinforcing to follow the sixteenth exercise with the internal statement "Letting Be," which evokes not just the sense of release in letting go but adds the sense of serenely witnessing whatever is there in consciousness. It is simply letting it be, not avoiding it, not identifying with it, not analyzing it. Whatever is happening, including the images and thoughts that keep flitting through the mind, just let them be, to flow on and pass by. The silent expression of the words, "letting be," can be repeated until you feel that you are really letting everything be just as it is. This, then, can be followed by the silent expression "just being," saying "just" with the inbreath and "being" with the outbreath. Just being means that you can rest serenely in being without having to "do" anything more. To reinforce this feeling, you can silently invoke the words "blessed being," for such a feeling and state of mind is certainly a blessing, a state in which the busy coming and goings of thoughts and impulses are in complete abeyance, and the mind is like a still, clear pool. To emphasize the sense of now, of being in the present, you can silently say "being here, here *now,*" and add such things as "here *now* in thanksgiving" (for the joy of *being* in the *now*) or "in peace, tranquility, serenity" to capture the sense of how it feels in the now.

It is quite helpful to use syllables or combinations of syllables subvocally for the in and out breaths of various steps in the sutra. For example, in the sixth step, after silently saying inwardly “Breathing in I can feel happy. Breathing out I can feel happy,” one can say “happy in” on the inbreath and “happy out” on the outbreath. That can be followed by breaking the word “happiness” into “happi” on the inbreath and “ness” on the outbreath. Silently repeating “happiness” in this manner can have an increasingly pleasant effect. In all of this it is pleasant and reinforcing to feel that as you let your breath out, it is gravity that is gently pulling it down, rather than your having to willfully push it down and out. Breathing then becomes something that is happening to you rather than your “doing” it. Breath is so central to this practice of meditation because it is the faculty that is simultaneously voluntary and involuntary. Thus, you can feel that you are breathing and, at the same time, that your breath is breathing you. In this sense, it becomes a bridge between the voluntary world and the involuntary world, where freedom and determinism become one and are no longer an issue. It is a most liberating place to be.

The crucial point about this meditation practice is its non-instrumental nature. It is not about achieving a distant goal, or being anywhere other than where you already are, which is resting in awareness. Consequently, whatever you are experiencing, pleasant or unpleasant, you are doing it right. If you are frightened, and are aware of it, you are doing it correctly. Even if you are confused, but know it, you are doing it right. The dimension of your consciousness that is aware of your confusion, doubt, pain, or other states of mind is not any of these states, and you can rest in that fundamental knowledge. Finally it should be emphasized that the sixteen steps in the above sutra cover core elements and teachings in Buddhist philosophy and psychology. They are the Four Establishments of the body, the feelings, the mind, and the objects of the mind, as mentioned earlier. The elements also cover the Seven Factors of Awakening, which are: (1) full attention, (2) investigating dharmas, (3) energy, (4) joy, (5) ease, (6) concentration, and (7) letting go.

In the beginning of meditative practice, we also have a strong sense of the body and its feeling of solidity; but as our practice goes on, our concentration gives us a more penetrating perception, in which we come to feel and know the body as an energy field with a continuous flow of sensations, and its fusion with the environmental energy field in and around us. In ancient China, the word *chi* was used to denote the vital breath or energy animating the universe. With the breath, we can imagine the rhythmic alternation of the two elemental forces of *yin* and *yang* coursing through the body, the environment, and even the cosmos, in a pattern of harmony and oneness. In the eleventh step of the sutra, on concentrating one's mind, it is helpful to concentrate both the mind and the body to sense the *chi* in the energy field that pulses and unifies you with your environment. This imaginative exercise during meditation can make a profound change in how we view ourselves, our environment, and how inclusively they are interconnected.

We have all been deeply conditioned by our upbringing, our culture, and our life experiences, so that there is a great deal of unconscious automaticity of thought and feeling in our minds at any one time. In fact, we can speak of a *collective* conditioning of the human mind. It is ubiquitous, universal, and difficult to get beyond. This is why it is so important to stay with the practice. By staying with it consistently, we recognize that we can rest in our being without getting so frequently trapped in the stream of our conditioned thoughts and feelings. We can be *present*, which is at the heart of contemplative being. When we realize while meditating that we are no longer attending to the breath, that realization itself is *presence*, and we are back in the present moment simply allowing the breath to again become the primary object of our attention.

Other Meditative Practices

Mindfulness meditation involves non-doing more that it involves doing anything. For this reason it has been called a "radical non-doing," which involves an inward stance of allowing and accepting rather than fixing or solving something. It is a way of being for its own sake rather than an instrumental method for achieving some outcome or purpose. However, there are some activities that are ordinarily instrumental in everyday life that can become excellent meditative practices in their own right. We could call them meditative "doings." Sitting meditation is traditionally carried out silently and without overt use of language, other than subvocal forms such as in the sutra or mantras. Yet, we find in both the East and the West there is a tradition and use of the written word as part of contemplative life and praxis. This goes very far back in the West, where the idea of an inner dialogue with oneself ultimately led to the literary genre of meditation by means of writing, in Marcus Aurelius' *Meditations*. Marcus observed that these are the kinds of things on which lovers of wisdom ought to meditate and that they ought to write down every day. Michel de Montaigne (1992) continued in this same spirit with his *Essays,* which are the product of a meditative introspection and inner dialogue that went well beyond the conventional attitudes and presuppositions of his time and society. His self-analysis and written exposition amounted to a deeply personal journal made public. When he retired at the age of thirty-eight, after an exemplary career as magistrate, counselor to kings, and Mayor of Bordeaux, he wanted to write, but was not sure what to write about, until he realized that he had retired in large part because of his dislike of all the pretensions and postures that people have to assume in public life. So he wrote with great honesty and directness about the workings of his own mind and body. He truly wrote as a man without any clothes on, about his eating, his defecating, his fornicating, his flatulence, and his sexual and other organs. This was done with a purpose—to deflate his and our images of ourselves as purely rational creatures who can ignore our basic bodily nature and functions, while aspiring to a totally cerebral life of the mind or spirit. And he pursued this deflation so that we would accept our frailties and cease claiming a mastery over our bodies and natural circumstances that we do not have; in short, he wanted us to come to accept ourselves as we are. So his philosophy was one of reconciliation with ourselves. As he wrote, "The most uncouth of our afflictions is to despise our being." Given that as a foundation, he proceeded to write some of the most insightful and revealing autobiographical literature since St. Augustine's *Confessions*. Thus, his writing was not only engaging but ultimately very humane. His *Essays*, as a form of candid self-reconciliation, can be seen as a forerunner of today's journal writing for the same purpose. Of course there have been journals written since that are fine literary products in their own right, as well as generated inspirational thought and ideas. In this regard, Emerson's journals certainly stand out, and Thoreau's *Walden* is one of the finest documents of this genre in American literature and philosophy. But the intent here is not to laud journal writing as a literary enterprise, but, rather, to describe its value for contemplative practice and aging.

It must be added at this point that the manual act of writing in long hand can itself be a meditative practice or "doing," and not only as part of a journal-writing process. Granted, our access to computers has diminished the use of handwriting substantially, but when done in a mindfully meditative way, handwriting is a rewarding form of contemplative practice. Meditative consciousness is a rich resource of images that resonate rather naturally in later life, and it is an excellent gateway to experiencing the manual act of writing as an aesthetic pastime in its own right. In its origins, writing is a form of drawing, which, after all, is a physical act of sketching or scratching by hand some physical form or figure on a receptive physical surface with some object of inscription, such as a chisel, a pencil, or a pen. Both the act and the resulting form or representation can provide a direct aesthetic experience that goes from one's hand to the page, without the intervention of a machine. One's handwriting does not have to be fine or elegant. True calligraphy is essentially the art of producing letters and words that capture the spirit of the experience or the text they represent. The same kind of effect can be had by careful attention to the physical act of writing itself. There is an expression in the beautiful tradition of Persian calligraphy that goes "Writing is the language of the hand, the idiom of the mind, the ambassador of the intellect, and the trustee of thought." The written word is essential to any spiritual system. From the Word of the Christian God, to the mysticism of the Kabbalah, to the sacred syllables of Tantric yogis, to the talismanic writings of the Taoists, the written word is central. In a truly contemplative state, the tip of the pen becomes the point of the mind. To write can be a sacred act.

Another form of contemplative practice based on the written word is the act of *reading*—not just reading sacred texts, but reading writings that deepen the contemplative mood and frame of mind. It is a venerable tradition and, according to Philo of Alexandria, *anagnosis* (reading) is one of the most essential contemplative exercises. In medieval Europe, the reading of sacred texts, or *Lectio Divina,* was an essential part of monastic practice. Even in our contemporary American culture, someone like Ram Dass (2000) claims that reading is an important element in his meditative practice. He feels that old age is a time for reflection and inner work, and that reading certain texts is a lifeline to wisdom. He goes to sources like the *Tao Te Ching*, the *Dhammapada: The Sayings of the Buddha*, and the *Bhagavad Gita* for inspiration in his practice. Substantively, one would do better to read Seneca's *On Peace of Mind* than the more contemporary Norman Vincent Peale's *Peace of Mind,* which wa written for a mass market. Yet there is much literature available to us today to enhance our contemplative practice, literature which enables us to gain insight about ourselves and our being that goes beyond the conventional forms, roles, and stereotypes of society. Thoreau's *Walden* carried that essential message—to pursue self knowledge in solitude and then to follow the fundamental laws of one's own being, without regard for custom, neighbors, nation, or church. Observing nature and reading great literature, he felt, would help one to discover these laws. There is a galaxy of great writers who are apt to put us into a contemplative or meditative state of mind. Poets like Wordsworth, Rilke, and Wallace Stevens immediately come to mind, but there are many, many others. Not only does such reading bring about a contemplative state of mind, but, more broadly, it reinforces one's contemplative practice and way of being.

Other forms of mindful meditative practice can be done in conjunction with art of any kind: painting, sculpture, music, and so on. This can involve viewing, listening to, and actually doing the art form itself. Listening to meditative music is a readily available practice. I find listening to Hayden's Symphony No. 20, "The Philosopher," to be highly meditative. Given the slow pulsation of its thematic movement, it is easy to imagine a solitary philosopher moving in slow, deliberate steps along a path, perhaps in the woods, in contemplation. As for doing art, painting a beautiful landscape (however inexpertly) can certainly be meditative in its doing. Apropos of landscapes, many elders become deeply, one can say meditatively, engrossed in gardening. They can become immersed in earth, planting, growth, decay, decomposition, and rebirth—all the basic rhythms and processes of nature. Movement can be another form of practice. Certain forms of dancing can be meditative. Certainly the movements of the Sufi dervishes can lead to ecstatic spiritual states. For elders, however, the gentle and flowing movements of Tai Chi can serve as an age-friendly meditative practice.

Practice as Process

Not only is the personal journal an effective vehicle for contemplative thought and expression, but it can be a meditative practice in its own right. Ira Progoff's (1975) intensive journal method is probably the most widely known approach to journal writing; and his later book, *The Prac-*

tice of Process Meditation (1980), has one of the clearest and most detailed expositions on meditative writing available. A key feature of this method is the inclusion of a relaxing meditative element that he calls "twilight imaging," because it takes place in the twilight state between waking and sleeping. In this state, the person follows the inward images and impressions with an open, undirected awareness, and simply observes them in a non-judgmental way as they present themselves. Workshop participants are asked to breathe slowly and softly in silence and let their thoughts drop away without thinking about them. They sit in quietness and calmness with their eyes closed, letting the softness of their breathing draw their eyelids together, and letting themselves quietly drift into the twilight level. After several minutes of this practice, they are asked to gather their impressions and observations from this level of consciousness and record them in a Twilight Imagery Log of their journals. What Progoff intends here is to create the conditions necessary for experiencing interiority and tapping into an underlying healing and creative process, which he believes is present in all of us.

What is different about Progoff's process meditation is that instead of simply observing the passing thoughts, images, and other contents, we are asked to gather our observations and record them in writing. We examine the images that appear, then we allow ourselves to become a bit more alert and jot those images down, and after that we return to the twilight state. Keep moving back and forth, jotting down the images. These are just jottings, not whole sentences, which would call for too much concentration and break the twilight nature of the experience. Note that this twilight state is not the alert awareness of mindfulness meditation, yet it is the most meditative of Progoff's journal procedures. Still, this level of consciousness is a rich resource for images that resonate rather naturally in later life, and it is an excellent gateway to experiencing the manual act of writing as an aesthetic pleasure in its own right.

It is important here to clarify the basic difference between process meditation and the various forms of sitting meditation, including the mindfulness form. In process meditation, one is alert to the passing images and thoughts that cross one's mind, and rather than simply observe them, one identifies and jots them down for further exploration and development. This calls for further reflection of a cognitive and conceptual nature, in order to record the content in meaningful sentences. Conversely, the initial problem in the practice of sitting meditation is to contend with the flux and flow of thought and other mental contents, to calm the jumping "monkey mind," and not get caught up in the contents. Indeed, the Zen Buddhist concept of no-mindedness, or no mind, and all texts on meditation, emphasize the need to slow down and empty the mind to the greatest extent possible. They warn against our tendency to glorify mind and, instead, see its incessant internal noise as an obstacle to finding the inner stillness that is a peace beyond understanding. This is the essence of their doctrine of *no-mind*. They feel that when Descartes believed he had found the most fundamental truth about being in the statement, "I think, therefore I am," he had in fact made the most basic error. Buddhists believe that enlightenment is, in large part, an end to the dreadful enslavement of incessant thinking, and thus the cessation of conflict and suffering caused by it. It is not necessary to be a Buddhist to recognize that when you meditate in silence and stillness thinking is calmed, and you can just watch without conflict or suffering. You don't have to think "I am watching;" for in nature, there can be watching without a separate watcher. Just watch whatever you are thinking, feeling, or experiencing. This is the essence of meditation as a process.

However, this is *not* to say that the life of the mind, in the intellectual sense, is out of the question as far as contemplative aging is concerned; far from it. One of the foremost modern contemplatives, Thomas Merton (1965), stated that rejecting the mind while proceeding along the path of illumination is "tantamount to spiritual suicide." If we come to believe that our *reason* is invalid, it deprives us of both our foremost instrument of guidance and the central means of collecting the fruit of our experience. Further, we are misled if we believe that the thoughts and images of our minds represent or mirror nature, for this sets us outside nature as mere spectators. Rather, our thoughts and ideas *are* nature, much like waves on the sea; so reason and mind should be honored and used intelligently as essential elements of human nature.

Contemplation, of course, goes beyond meditation. What we know of consciousness today is that we engage in a continual process of constructing and reconstructing our perceptions of what is actual and "real." The idea of "reality," in what is called "normal" consciousness, raises important issues. Normal reality is a consciousness that can be shown through sensory experimentation to be a constructed reality. In order to

...age the many stimuli impinging on our consciousness from the environment, we develop a mental sensory-filtering system from childhood, and it is continually shaped by subsequent situations and conditioning. What is experienced as reality is actually a representation and not the thing itself. So, if "normal" consciousness is constructed, then it can be altered by changing the manner or the frame of its construction. In this way new insight, epiphanies, and even mystical experiences can be seen as forms of transcendence of normal consciousness, and a reintegration based on the knowledge gained from the experience.

Our normal consciousness has been called the "invented reality" (Watzlawick, 1984). We often refer to normal consciousness as common sense, and we assume that reality can be *discovered* by it. However, the modern theory of *constructivism* postulates that what we call reality is a particular way of looking at the world, based on our individual development and situation in the world as shaped by family, society, culture, and so on (Berger & Luckman, 1967; Learning-Theories.com, 2010; Pinker, 2002). Therefore, it can be said that reality is literally invented or constructed, but not discovered. Not only individual, but social, scientific, and ideological "realities" are constructed and naively assumed to be the "real" realities. One of the most profound statements in this regard is that we do not see things as they are; we see things as we are. It should be apparent that if meditation and contemplative practice alters our way of perceiving things, alters our frame of consciousness, then it could conceivably change our whole view of reality.

The likelihood is that such a change can be the result of an ongoing process of meditation that opens the mind and body to new experiences, rather than the result of a sudden flash of insight, illumination, and transformation. Practice, then, means learning to let the in-dwelling experience of being emerge. The process of meditation can take us inward to such an extent that there is no longer any inside or outside. One feels like an intrinsic part or feature of a larger process, which is very much like what was referred to as cosmic consciousness in the theory of gerotranscendence. But is this an experience of transcendence or immanence?

The Telos of Practice

The theory of gerotranscendence identifies an increased "feeling of cosmic union with the spirit of the universe" (Tornstam, 2005, p. 4) as a key feature and outcome of psychological and spiritual development in later life. As an outcome, this is like a transcendent goal or *telos* of the aging process. This wording, "cosmic union with the spirit of the universe," seems almost celestial and unearthly, transcending this mortal coil. It makes one think of looking up at the sky and galaxies in awe and reverence, and having feelings of deliverance from this known, troublesome world below. Yet, indwelling, rather than looking outward and upward, has been the stance of most of the contemplative approaches presented so far in this chapter. Consequently, one thinks of this stance as one of deep internal immersion in meditation or prayer. This indwelling has been described here as natural to the elderly, and it is interesting that Quakers, whose whole focus is on the inner spirit, use the term "eldering" to describe a process by which they very gently and respectfully counsel those who appear to have lost the way. The way is through the inner spirit rather than an other-worldly or heavenly spirit.

Spiritual experience can be both transcendent and immanent, in that it can be an experience of transcending worldly concerns as well as an intensely grounded experience, in which it feels as though the ground of being has been reached for at least one precious moment. Thus, we can have *ascenders* and *descenders*, according to this view. Given the process conception of practice just presented, it is hard to see the possibility in this life of ascending to a totally quiescent, peaceful, and lasting state of transcendence. This points to an ancient ontological difference between Parmenides and Heraclitus. Parmenides thought the changing perceptible world was one of appearance only, whereas there is a "real," unchanging, and eternal intelligible world beyond it, a nirvana. Heraclitus, of course, saw all reality in this world as being in continual flux and change.

The process view would seem to favor the route of immanence. It proposes that we are part and parcel of a larger, universal energic process and, if we do not try to separate an eternal soul from a material body in a mind-body dualism, there is still the possibility of a divine ground of being, which is immanent and accessible to consciousness in the midst of this changing, perceptible world. Through practice, the mind becomes reembodied in a way it has not been since infancy. Sights, sounds, sensations in and through the body become mysteriously fresh and new. Yet we recognize that every aspect of these experiences comes and goes when we are indwelling in full awareness of the entire field of our mind-body experience. With each in-breath and out-breath, thoughts, feelings, desires, and aversions emerge along with sights, smells, tastes, and impulses passing in a mixed potage. Full awareness of the constant comings and goings permits us to see the impermanence of our impulses, desires, and fears, just as in the sutra of mindfulness meditation we observe the impermanence of all *dharmas*, all phenomena. Yet, paradoxically, as we cultivate a familiarity and intimacy with these passing things in this open awareness, we come to appreciate more deeply, even reverently, what we see, touch, taste, smell, and hear. Things take on a new aura, a numinous quality that was not there before. This lends a quite mysterious quality to the simple activities of everyday life—life's everyday mysticism—such as getting up in the morning, bathing, clothing, and feeding one's self, doing those things reverently and with presence of mind rather than routinely. Thus, at any moment we can come in touch with our wholeness, our completeness, in a full acceptance of things as they are, whether good, bad, or indifferent. Such a state of mind takes us beyond good and bad, liking and disliking, and definitely beyond appearance. Hence, we can sense and actually experience, at least intermittently, that still state of peace, tranquility, and serenity that Parmenides saw as beyond appearance.

Perhaps the best metaphorical term for such a state within a process scenario of change and flux is the "eye." Thus, we speak of the "eye of the storm" as that utterly motionless state of tranquility in the center of a swirling maelstrom. It is interesting to see the correspondence of "I" to "eye" at this level of consciousness. William James (1985) notes that when you use the word "I" it is really a word of position, like "here" or "this." It is a position within the universe, like Emerson's (1990, p.18) famous "eyeball" in his essay *Nature*: "Standing on the bare ground . . . all mean egotism vanishes. I become a transparent eyeball; I am nothing; I see all; the currents of the Universal Being circulate through me; I am part or particle of God." Thus, each of us is an aperture through which the universe looks at itself.

Given a process orientation toward ourselves and our lives, contemplative practice *is* a telos or end in itself. Meditation, in particular, has been presented here as a form of being in itself. Yet it is important to add that meditation, and notably mindfulness meditation, has been used effectively for clinical purposes in the fields of applied psychology, psychiatry, and social work. The psychological healing effects of mindfulness have been known to some practitioners for more than four decades (Dearthage, 1979), but it has become more prominent in the recent clinical literature and practice (Baer, 2006; Germer, Siegel, & Fulton, 2005; Hayes, Follette, & Linahan, 2004; Sherman & Siporin, 2008). Perhaps the most widely-known current application of the mindfulness approach is being carried on in the Center for Mindfulness in Medicine, Health Care and Society at the University of Massachusetts Medical School. This program has been adopted and is in use in many medical institutions across the country. Jon Karat-Zinn (2009), a clinical psychologist, established the Stress Reduction Program in the Center, which is the oldest and largest stress reduction program of its kind in the country. It uses mindfulness meditation and mindful practices in helping patients deal with chronic pain associated with medical conditions, as well as managing stress that impedes healthy body-mind functioning in general. Kabat-Zinn's approach goes beyond the use of meditation to obtain a relaxation response, and incorporates the psycho-spiritual foundation of mindfulness practice, as outlined by Thich Nhat Hanh (1975) and others in that contemplative tradition.

I have found that mindfulness meditation as part of a total treatment approach is particularly helpful in dealing with reactive depression, which is the most widely diagnosed psychiatric condition among older adults. One of the most demoralizing of the reactive depressions occurs in elders who have been diagnosed as having Alzheimer's disease. A friend and colleague in gerontology described the tragic situation of a group of retired professors who were in a project he designed, to try to help them deal with their diagnoses of early and mid-stage Alzheimer's. The tragic effects of having that particular disease in persons dedicated to the life of the mind became very evident in witnessing aged academics who were undergoing the ravages of Alzheimer's disease on their brains. The most highly valued aspect of their identities and way of life was under deadly assault. It has occurred to me and some others that there may be no better way to prepare oneself intellectually and emotionally for the loss of one's mind and one's self in a dementia like Alzheimer's than by meditation practice. The daily practice of emptying the mind in meditation provides the experience of letting go of memory as well other mental contents in a gentle, peaceful way. It also provides a more benign, less frightening view of what that mental state might be like, if it should arrive. Ram Dass (2000, p. 38), formerly known as Richard Alpert, gives a winsome description of one of his visits to his eighty-six year old aunt with late-life dementia. His conversation with her went as follows:

> She: "What's your name?"
> He: "Richard."
> She: "Who's your father?"
> He: "Your brother George."
> She: "Oh, yes, yes." (long pause) "Are you and I the same age?"
> He: "No."
> She: "Am I older than you?"
> He: "Yes, you're thirty years older than I am."
> She: "*Thirty years* older? But you're all gray!"
> He: "So are you!"
> She: (long pause) "What did you say your name was?"

He added: "And around we'd go again. My aunt was just floating out there, with little connection to time or personal relationships. Most often I held her hand, and we looked into each other's eyes. It didn't matter that she couldn't remember me; she didn't seem particularly anxious about it. We were just two beings in Soul time together. . . . both of us enjoyed our visits immensely" (p. 38). He noted further that we all become so identified with our thoughts and feelings, and that they tell us who we are, that it is hard not to panic when our minds slip; but the loss of our cognitive faculties need not be so frightening. He had suffered a massive cerebral hemorrhage with only ten percent chance of survival just three years prior to publishing his book *Still Here*, in which he related the above conversation with his aunt. So he was writing from authentic personal experience about physical assaults on the mind. Yet years of meditative practice were central to his equanimity in dealing with the terrible effects of his stroke.

Alzheimer's and other late life dementias are going to increase as the Baby Boom and later generations go into later adulthood and live longer and longer. We can hope for possible medical treatments and, perhaps, cures of these conditions through stem cell and other research. In the meantime, a contemplative later life with meditation at its core can do a great deal to mitigate their devastating psychological effects. The transcending feature of all this is that meditation is a way of being in itself, which can last as long as the mind itself. By letting go of the contents of the mind every day in practice, we can less frighteningly let go of the mind itself.

Chapter Six

Imaginative Aging

Dictionaries give several definitions of the word "imagination." They all describe it generally as the act or power of forming mental images of what is not physically present at the moment. Some also describe it as the act or power of creating images of what has never been actually experienced, and of creating new images or ideas by combining previous experiences. The latter is described as *creative power* and, therefore, distinguished from *fancy*. Imagination is a more deeply creative faculty, in that it perceives the basic resemblances between things, whereas fancy is a lighter faculty that perceives superficial resemblances. Imagination is also a form of mental activity that is distinct from cognitive or intellectual processes—more of a free creative use of the mind and its images. This latter description captures more of the form and the spirit of what is meant in this chapter by imaginative aging.

The Primacy of the Image

The image is so fundamental to all human experience that it passes without recognition in our everyday lives. Yet, as Gregory Bateson (1980) notes in his book *Mind and Nature*, all conscious perception has image characteristics, and this is because our brains make the images of what we think we perceive directly. In this sense, all experience is subjective. As he describes the experience of pain, for example, he notes that it is located somewhere; it has a beginning and an end; and the location stands out against a background. These are the elementary components of any image. If someone steps on my toe, what I experience is not the person stepping on my toe, but my *image* of someone stepping on my toe. This image is reconstructed from neural reports reaching my brain immediately following that person's foot landing on mine. This experience is subjective because all experience of the exterior is always mediated through interior sense organs and neural pathways, not directly. Thus, objects are something of my own inner creation, and my experience of them is not truly objective; it is undeniably subjective. Furthermore, the *processes* of perception are inaccessible to consciousness and only the *products* are conscious. These products, of course, are necessary for both our basic survival and everyday lives. However, since we are not conscious of the process of making the images we consciously see, we use a whole range of presuppositions that become built into the finished image. We ordinarily take this to be empirical knowledge. Although it is known that the image we "see" is manufactured by the mind, or in the brain, we tend to take this as the actual "thing-in-itself," Kant's *Ding-an-sich*.

One problem with the dictionary definitions of imagination is that the words "the act or *power* of forming mental images" gives the impressions of a proactive, willful procedure. Kenneth Boulding (1987), in his informative and insightful book *The Image*, claims that it is not likely that the unconscious aspect of the image can be brought into conscious view by a simple act of will. This is because the process by which images are formed involves so much filtering, based not only on survival priorities but also on prior training and experience, as well as censoring and repression. It has become automated and habitual. There have been empirical studies of the process of "de-automatization," by which these automatic and delimiting features give way to a more open and inclusive mode of consciousness (Deikman, 1966). By assuming an open and receptive attitude toward mental content, as in meditation or the phenomenological reduction method, a perceptual expansion occurs, in which awareness includes stimuli that are usually filtered out or habitually denied consciousness. As these information-limiting processes are de-automatized, the boundaries of the mind expand to include a wider source of insight and information. In this de-automatized, receptive mode, we are able to see beyond or reconcile differences, and are able to tolerate paradox and other apparent contraries. Thus, we are open to new and creative knowledge. This same phenomenon has also been used to explain the unusual sensations associated with mystical experiences. It is the mode of perception that has changed, not the external stimuli themselves. We have all experienced this kind of phenomenon with regard to time. We may experience a minute as fleeting or it may appear to drag on endlessly. Yet, "normal" clock time would be identical in both instances.

In the receptive mode, seeing softens into a beholding gaze, which allows greater freedom of arrival and passage of images and impressions. To use William Blake's phrase, we "cleanse the doors of perception." Thus, we can see anew with the freshness, openness, and awe of a child.

Studies of eidetic imagery in children show that, compared to adults, their imagery and thought (1) are more vivid and sensuous, (2) are syncretic, (3) are physiognomic and animated, (4) soften the distinctions between self and object and between objects, and (5) display greater fusion of sense modalities. What happens in the course of development and social conditioning is that images change in functional character. They are more often shaped largely by the demands and exigencies of abstract thought, and once the image changes its function, it becomes an instrument of reflective and abstract processes. As the abstraction process and function develop further, the sensuousness, the fullness of detail, and the color and vividness of the image necessarily fade. However, if this process is reversed by de-automatization practices, such as deep meditation, a phenomenon of unity emerges, particularly in reported mystic experiences. The unity phenomenon is one in which all boundaries are merged until the self is no longer experienced as a separate object, and conventional perceptual and cognitive distinctions are no longer applicable to the experience.

Automatization can be seen as a way of abstracting ourselves mentally from the pulsating world and universe, in order to have some sense of control over it and over ourselves in it. But the self is in the world and the world is in the self. As Bateson puts it, the mental system that governs how we think and learn is the very same sort of system that governs the evolution and ecology of all life on earth. He sees a "meta-pattern" that connects every living thing on this planet. This is remarkable because Bateson comes to this conclusion from an empirical and scientific position, yet it sounds very much like the Buddhist concept of *Interbeing*, in which all things and beings are related to each other in a pulsating web or system of interconnections. Consequently, there is a reverence for all things in this great "network of being" for Buddhists. From this point of view, our minds are not separated from other minds and the external world, because it is all one process. Nature is all of a piece and everything in it goes with everything else. There is also just one energy that pulsates in an on-and-off manner, in which being and not-being, consciousness and unconsciousness, and life and death are its dynamic polarities.

Alfred North Whitehead, who was a scientific thinker of the first rank, came to a conclusion very similar to the Interbeing and meta-pattern concepts. He speaks of a "mutual immanence" in the experience of ourselves as both *in* and *of* the world. He also speaks of "prehension," which is an apprehension by the senses of a unity and ultimate harmony in the world. This, of course, is not unlike the claim of Spinoza and Leibniz in the West and the Taoists in the East. In fact, what the Taoists speak of metaphorically as the Tao is very much like what Bateson speaks of as a meta-pattern, in his more declarative, scientific voice.

Images come before words and language in an evolutionary and psychological sense; and, in effect, words are abstract symbols or representations of images or image constellations. Words and language put boundaries around much of our streaming mental content and, of course, they perform the function of cultural and societal shaping and conditioning of the individual's thinking and behavior. By receptive de-automatization processes, such as meditation, these boundaries can be loosened. Process meditation, with its twilight imaging, is an excellent example of this. Ira Progoff (1980) developed process meditation out of his familiarity with a technique developed by Jung, called "active imagination." Parenthetically, it should be noted that Progoff studied under Jung as a Bollingen Fellow in Switzerland. Jung used this technique by encouraging his patients to enter a state of reverie, in which judgment was suspended but consciousness preserved, and imagination was allowed to remain active. He also encouraged his patients to draw or paint their fantasies derived from this state, in order to recover hidden parts of themselves. These hidden parts, he felt, would in all likelihood emanate from the person's unconscious archetypal images. Jung used this therapeutic method of artistic rendering on himself to cope with his own psychosis. The results can be seen in the posthumously named *The Red Book* (2009) that his family recently allowed to be made public, which is replete with Jung's writings and ornate, surreal drawings that reflect his dreamlife and archetypal fantasies. Jung claimed that the archetype is an "irrepresentable, unconscious, pre-existent form" that seems to be part of the inherited structure of the psyche. It is a primordial image and instinctual in nature, so it can manifest itself spontaneously anytime and anywhere. However, parts of that unconscious and amorphous image are more likely to arise experientially in a relaxed, receptive state such as active imagination or process meditation. That is because parts or pre-existent traces of the image are the *a priori* inborn forms of intuition, and of perception and apprehension. The drawing or painting of images from these parts and traces were then used in the psychotherapy to enhance the process of individuation—which means becoming a single, homogeneous being, in the sense of becoming one's own self. Individuation has, therefore, been translated as "coming to selfhood" or "self-realization" (Storr, 1983). Gathering "the parts" from these receptive states brings to mind Emerson's observation that each of us has to "contemplate his own proper nature," which could well mean introspection on those parts and traces of the primordial image of the self. On this view, the extent to which our active imagination arises in the form of archetypal images, the more creative and authentic will our imaginative aging be. This is a different process than recollecting the self from past behaviors and events in the usual reminiscing of later life.

Reflective Imagery

Thus we live on images, whether we are aware of it or not. This seems to be the case the older we get. These recollective images are not so much in the form of exact memories, e.g., of specific events and people, as much as they are a montage of fused images. These inchoate images come first, and then we have to work consciously to construct a full image memory of the person, place, or event. This calls for some reflection, and this is what is meant by reflective imagery. This is a process that is pleasurable and replenishing in its own right as well as creative in its potential. Milton Glazer, the legendary graphic designer, disdained the graphics of the computer and, at age seventy-five, observed that the computer is finite in its decisions whereas the mind is fuzzy. Fuzziness, he stated, is "an essential quality of the imagination." As Jung (1965, p. 320) wrote in his own old age, "With increasing age, contemplation, and reflection, the inner images naturally play an even greater part in man's life. 'Your old men shall dream dreams. . . .' In old age one begins to let memories unroll before the mind's eye and, musing, to recognize oneself in the inner and outer images of the past."

What Jung is referring to is reverie and its particular relevance to the quality of being in later life. Humans have always fashioned reveries out of sights, sounds, odors, tastes, and memories. As the French philosopher Gaston Bachelard (1971, p. 102) once wrote, "The being of reverie crosses all ages of man from childhood to old age without growing old."

Bachelard developed a phenomenological method for the study of reverie, and found that that the spontaneous appearance in consciousness of an image begins a process, or what he describes as "a sudden salience on the surface of the psyche," which consumes our entire being, however briefly. He refers to this as the "poetic image" that represents a basic process of the human imagination, which is not restricted to poets or artists. However, one must be receptive to the image at the moment it appears, for the poetic image is sudden and transient. The phenomenology of the poetic imagination goes beyond trying to identify and solidify images in memories that can be dated in time. As Bachelard describes the poetic image, it is experienced as a fluid "intimacy of fusion." In his words, "with intimacy it recovers its entity, in the mellowness and imprecision of the inner life." It is as though something fluid gathers our memories and we become "dissolved in this fluid of the past." He contends that for knowledge of this intimacy, localization in the spaces of our intimacy is more urgent than the identification of dates. However, the fragments of past images that come together in our imagination should be allowed to happen, to merge into a larger image from diverse moments and places. Finally, Bachelard (1971, p. 23) has an interesting relevance for the theory of gerotranscendence and the prominent place of cosmic consciousness in it when he writes, "At the end, imagining a cosmos is the most natural destiny of reverie."

James Hillman (1999), too, felt that the last years of life were so valuable for reviewing life, for "cosmological speculations," and for sensory enjoyment of the "world's images." As he puts it in *The Force of Character*, the soul is replenished by the richness of images, as well as absorbed into another imagination that goes beyond the limits of one's actual condition. Yet when it comes to memories and reminiscence, it is wise not to get stuck in the past with static and repetitive recalling or ruminating. As Jung (1965, p. 320) expressed this in his *Memories, Dreams, Reflections*, "The images keep me from getting lost in personal retrospection. Many old people become too involved in their reconstruction of past events. They remain imprisoned in these memories. But if it is reflective and is translated into images, retrospection can become *reculer pour mieux sauter.*" Jung's use of this French phrase captures the sense in which imaginative, non-grasping reflection on memories or shards of memories makes for a better savoring, for a finer and more tasteful appreciation of them. For the reality is that there is no recollection without context, and since context in the present is constantly changing, there can never be a fixed or absolute memory. Memory without the present cannot exist, so what we do is actively engage in constructing or reconstructing memories out of shards and fragments of the past in the present. Since this is the case, it does us well, as Jung suggests, to bring our *present* sensitivities and imagination into play in letting our "memories unroll before the mind's eye and, musing, to recognize oneself in the inner and outer images of the past."

For Marcus Aurelius, all images are suitable if they strike the imagination and make one conscious of the illusions and conventions of mankind. Becoming aware of the illusory nature of so many of our conventional concerns and constraints can enlighten us and lessen much of our existential angst. When this happens, not by philosophical analysis, but by a revelatory image or experience, the results are truly illuminating and lasting. This was brought home to me compellingly by a seventy-nine year old man during an interview of him I was taping for a study of the role that reminiscence plays in later life. He related an incident, an epiphany actually, which profoundly affected him at a particularly difficult time of his life. He was forty-one at the time and had just recently received notice of the finalization of his divorce, which his wife had initiated and he accepted after several attempts at reconciliation. In the midst of the emotional turmoil brought on by their separation and ensuing divorce, he decided to accept a new job offer in New York City and to leave the suburban area in eastern Pennsylvania where he and his wife had lived for their ten years of marriage.

He had hoped the move and the change would help him to deal with the emotional turmoil and feelings of depression caused by the breakup. But he found the offices of his new employer were in temporary quarters in preparation for a move to a final location in a newly constructed office building in Manhattan, which furthered the mental turmoil and his depressed mood. He found himself sharing the same office with two other people surrounded by packing boxes and files, awaiting the move to the new location. Because of the transient nature of the office situation, he was not finding it possible to begin cementing friendships with his new co-workers. He was feeling intensely lonely, not only in Manhattan where he had no friends to speak of, but lonely in his life generally. His marriage had been childless and he had no surviving siblings, so his only close relatives were his elderly parents and they lived in the Midwest.

One day, during this dispiriting period of his life, and during a lunch break from his temporary workplace, he walked to nearby Central Park and sat down on a bench under some trees adjoining the Metropolitan Museum of Art. Having finished his lunch, he began reading a book that had been recommended to him by one of his new co-workers. The book was entitled, simply, *The Book*, by Alan Watts (1966). He recalled watching and listening to a few talks by Watts a number of years before on television from some station in San Francisco, and he remembered being bothered by Watts' smooth and unruffled delivery. The fact that Watts was always dressed in a kimono, and with a Japanese tea set invariably in front of him, was also irritating to him for some reason. However, the book was an inexpensive and short little paperback, so he felt he had nothing to lose by trying to read it.

Yet when he began reading it under the trees on that particularly balmy afternoon, he found himself becoming deeply engrossed in the book, while intensely aware of his natural surroundings in a peculiarly simultaneous way. Watts' words were carrying him into an unexpectedly lightened mood and frame of mind. He soon found himself without any sense of self-awareness or self boundaries, not of his skin, his clothes, or anything separating him from his immediate surroundings or anything beyond. Rather, he felt unbounded and "at one with everything." The fact that he was on a lunch break was lost to him, for he was enveloped in a feeling of timelessness. As an educated and widely-read man, he hesitated to say it, because it was a cliché, but he had to say that the experience was *transformative*. He devoured the remainder of the book later that same evening. It changed his outlook on many things from that time on, and he read and reread *The Book* a number of times over the ensuing years. He went through several copies, underlining, highlighting, and writing in the margins until the paperback bindings gave way and the pages became dog-eared. If ever there was a testimonial to Ram Dass' advice about the value of reading spiritually enlightening books, this was it. However, this man was very clear that it was the recollected *image* of that transformative experience that served him so well during the later years of his life. In his low periods, he could conjure up that image of himself in Central Park and his spirits would be lifted. The image was like a talisman for him.

As remarkable as this experience was, it was even more remarkable to me, because a number of years before hearing of his experience from reading *The Book*, I heard about an almost diametrically opposite effect on a young man while he was reading the same book. This young man had applied for treatment in a center for psychotherapy in a northeastern city, and he was assigned to me for short-term counseling. He applied because he was feeling a great deal of stress and psychological distress, as a graduate student in anthropology at a nearby university. He felt that he needed a course of therapy to carry him through the twin pressures of completing the last of his doctoral courses and getting his dissertation proposal approved by a committee of faculty yet to be selected. He was twenty-eight years old at that time, and he informed me that he had missed some significant educational time in the course of his undergraduate years, because he was hospitalized with a diagnosis of schizophrenia when he was 19 years old. The remarkable thing to me was when he commented that the schizophrenic break occurred while he was reading Watts' *The Book*! As he described it, Watts' writing seemed to mesmerize him and make him feel that he had "lost all boundaries." He could no longer distinguish inside from outside, and found that to be intensely confusing and frightening. This set off a process in which he even began to hear voices that seemed to come from the outside, telling him upsetting things. He realized, as a result of his treatment, that the voices were his own inner projections to the outside. But at that time, he was not able to function in any rational sense and had to be hospitalized.

How could it be that in the case of the middle-aged man reading *The Book*, it led to a positive life transformation, and in the case of the late adolescent, it lead to a schizophrenic breakdown? As I pondered this after hearing the older man's narrative, it began to make some sense to me. From a psychoanalytic point of view, the ego of a person with schizophrenia is weak and unable to withstand the dilemmas posed by reality (Freud, 1995). Perception and judgment are poor, as is reality testing. This is because the ego boundaries are diffuse and ill-formed, causing outer reality to be threatening to any sense of integrity and self-identity. The kind of feeling this young man was experiencing when reading *The Book* amounted to a fear of losing himself. For the person with schizophrenia, this is the *fear of annihilation* (Semrad, 1960). The ings of cosmic consciousness in an older person with a reas ego are blissful feelings, whereas for younger persons vulnerab phrenic breaks such feelings can lead to overwhelming fear o hilation of self.

This young man was ripe for such a breakdown when he read *The Book*. He tried to recall some of the statements in it that particularly upset him, but he was having difficulty trying to recall any. In order to gain some insight into this, I made a point of reading the book myself. The first thing that struck me was that the writing was clear and compelling, and that the book was hard to put down. But then there were specific passages that I immediately recognized as potentially threatening to someone in the mental state of this young man. One such passage was the following: "You will thus realize that you—as ego—are a fake. You will feel like an onion: skin after skin, subterfuge after subterfuge, is pulled off to find no kernel at the center. Which is the whole point: to find out that the ego is indeed a fake—a wall of defense around a wall of defense . . . around nothing" (Watts, 1966, p. 114).

On the other hand, passages such as the following, in all likelihood, could lead to transcendence-like feelings in the older man:

> How is it possible that a being with such sensitive jewels as the eyes, such enchanted musical instruments as the ears, and such a fabulous arabesque of nerves as the brain can experience itself as anything less than a god? And when you consider that this incalculably subtle organism is inseparable from the still more marvelous patterns of its environment—from the minutest electrical designs to the whole company of the galaxies—how is it conceivable that this incarnation of all eternity can be bored with *being*? (Watts, 1966, p. 128)

This passage, too, would be terribly threatening to the young man, for it can loosen the sense of self (ego) boundaries. Fortunately, fragile, pre-psychotic egos are much more the exception than the rule in young persons, and they are much less common among older persons who have never suffered from schizophrenic breaks. Cosmic consciousness in later life is much more a gift than a threat.

ɪme Art

This process of rolling over or re-viewing a memory, or trace of a memory, in one's imagination can be made into a kind of art form. The term *time art* is one I coined, to describe certain unanticipated and unusual things I found in both research and clinical practice involving reminiscence and life review experiences among older adults. It is a phenomenon that is very much in line with Jung's observation about inner images playing an ever greater role in the later years of life, but for some elders it has also become something of an art form. Actually, imagination is "a necessary element in true recollection," as Ernst Cassirer (1944) once observed, and by this he meant recollection as a truly aesthetic experience. The ancient Greeks developed an art of memory, which was later passed on to Rome and then to the rest of Europe. The art involved the manipulation of images in memory using actual architectural and spatial contexts as visual backdrops, which served as mnemonic devices for the storage and retrieval of information from the past. While this had an archival function, it was nevertheless an art. John Dewey (1934) noted, in his highly influential *Art as Experience*, that in a work of art different acts, occurrences, and operations melt and fuse into a unity, and still do not lose their own character as they do so. The existence of this unity is assured and constituted by a single *quality* that pervades the entire experience, despite the variation of its constituent parts. It was precisely this unity of recollection that made for the archival value of those ancient artists of memory. Surely the aesthetic element of their art applies to recollection more generally, as Cassirer maintained.

Proust's (1981) recollection of tasting the madeleine at his grandparents' home, in the fictional town of Combray, became one of the most enduring examples of memory as an art form in all of Western literature. It was the ineffable quality of that taste that provided the unity and the timelessness of that experience, never to be forgotten. There is something about human consciousness that allows for the experience of timelessness. Hans Castorp, in Thomas Mann's *The Magic Mountain* (1995), found that the ordered and managed time of his business life was slipping away from him, in his stay at the TB sanatorium in the Swiss Alps. There he found himself drifting into a kind of timelessness, where all temporal measures disappear and time loses its shape. This slippage of his normal sense of measured time became the essential condition of a deeper experience, which opened another dimension of life for him.

Although Castorp drifted into this state, others have found that it is readily available to our imagination, and that through it time becomes malleable. At age 83, Bernard Berenson (1963) observed, "I can't believe it not worth living, for an infinity of ideated sensations remain in memory to be combined and recombined in charming ways." More prosaically, Thoreau observed that "time is but the stream I go a-fishing in." In effect Thoreau was making fun of the conventionally linear way we view time. If you think about it, there are several permutations of past→present→future, if you are willing to rearrange those three periods in reversed or mixed sequences. Take, for example, Heidegger's (1927) observation that "our past comes to meet us out of the future." Flaubert recognized the pleasure of anticipation, but observed that years later it is "not the memory of the deed, but the memory of past anticipations" that is the most rewarding. I have on several occasions had the experience, while driving along the Hudson River, of anticipating in my imagination arriving at and savoring a beloved place on the River. When I arrive there, I do indeed have the experience of a remembered present. Robert Edelman (1989), a neuro-scientist, wrote a book entitled *The Remembered Present*, in which he claims that the biology that creates consciousness does so by recovering the past in the present, comparing the past with the present, and re-storing the modified conception. There could be a good deal of imagination in that comparison of past with the present. From another sort of mixed time perspective, I recall hearing a commentator make the following cogent observation about a book by Tom Wolfe: Wolfe looks back derisively from a not-too-distant future on contemporary American fashion, wealth, and sexual behavior. From a scientific point of view, it can be added that relativity theory indicates that each individual has his or her own personal measure of time, and that the uncertainty principle of quantum mechanics indicates time is fluid rather than fixed.

The various time permutations of memories and anticipations in one's present awareness frequently have an almost playful quality in later life, when the conventional, linear view of time begins to loosen, and images begin to blend and meld in fanciful ways. There is an interesting exercise in which, as you enter into different situations in the course of a day, you look upon each one as having already happened. In other words, you look upon every detail as predetermined. This is not really different from treating your life as a play that has already been written, and you are an actor rehearsing your part. Although there is an element of amusement and playfulness in this exercise, if you really work at it, you begin to feel something of a very different quality emerging. You begin to feel, in a subtle and gentle way, that you are being liberated, and if you continue with this exercise, you begin to realize that there is something illusory about you as well as about time. Your old feelings of being in control and utterly responsible for yourself and your future are replaced with a feeling of being freed from and seeing through the egoistic self, with all its plans and socially conditioned concerns and obsessions. Ancient contemplative traditions, which tell us that time is illusory, are also telling us that we are immersed in illusions about ourselves. The quality of the experience resulting from this exercise makes for a unity that would be considered art by John Dewey (1934). This fits his claim that the aesthetic aspect of the experience is receptive and involves surrender, but that "adequate yielding of the self is possible only through a controlled activity that may well be intense." This exercise does call for an intensity of concentration and, while it is a form of imaginative art, it yields a remarkable ontological shift in one's consciousness as well. It involves a move to lightness and freedom from anxious, egoistic efforts at self-control and self-determination.

Our capacity for being able to manipulate time in our imagination and make it experientially real lies in the encompassing consciousness behind all our perceptions, prehensions, and preconceptions. Kant claimed that all experience must conform to knowledge, and our only way of perceiving and knowing the world, or "reality," is in terms of time and space. There is a tendency, however, for humans to conflate time and space, and we tend to spatialize time into states or categories such as past (behind), present (here), and future (in front of). Additionally, we habitually use this particular linear sequence over and over again. Finally, we quantify these time-spaces both linguistically (long ago, a short while ago) and mathematically (ten years ago, ten seconds ago). This is, of course, immensely valuable and practical for planning our many human activities and projects. Yet it is habitual and it is not cast in bronze. The consciousness that enabled Tolstoy at 81 to see himself "exactly the same way" as he was at age five or six is a prior, and more encompassing one, than our habitual consciousness. However, this consciousness cannot be its own object, as Sartre contended. In this respect, it is like an eye, an object that cannot observe itself by itself. This might give us the sense of what God's encompassing vision could conceivably be, and this sense led Oscar Wilde to comment that the past, present, and future are but "one moment in the sight of God" and that "the imagination can transcend them." Here again Karl Jaspers' compelling concept of the *Encompassing* comes to mind.

Henri Bergson (1922) claimed that "real time" is experienced as duration (*duree*), which is the form that the succession of our conscious states assumes when our intellect refrains from separating its present state from its former states. Real time, *duree*, is apprehended by intuition, not through separate operations of the intellect. Instead, what we do is project time into a spatial sense of duration, which makes succession in the stream of consciousness take the form of a continuous line or chain, in which the parts touch but never penetrate one another. This categorical spacing and division of time prevents the experience of *duree* and the eternal. The ability to experience *duree* can be a sublime aesthetic and spiritual element in contemplative practice.

For St. Augustine, neither the past nor the future seemed to exist, because "the past no longer is, and the future has not yet come to be." The present alone is actual, in this sense. He spoke of time as a three-fold present: the present as we experience it, as present memory, and the future as present expectation. This provides a clue to dealing with one of the dilemmas of contemplative practice, i.e., how to maintain the preeminence of the present, the Now, in the stream of consciousness. The problem is how one can apprehend or remain in the present, whether in meditation or in thought, in view of what James called the *specious* present. It no sooner arrives than it is gone, so it is specious to say it is here in any measurable sense. The key word in this, of course, is "measurable." Since we conventionally and habitually give the meaning of time this extensivity, we invariably experience it as fleeting, at best.

The answer lies in the intuitive recognition by Augustine of the transtemporality of the present. The past is always remembered in the present and the future is always anticipated or imagined in the present. It is recognition of this simultaneity that not only enables us to imagine it but put it into practice as well. In meditation, for example, when memories or anticipations intrude there could be a tendency to try to willfully exclude them in order to remain in the preferred present. Of course, this is contrary to sound meditative practice, which is to allow the contents of consciousness to arise and recede while simply observing them. By implicitly recognizing that all content of the past and the future must *necessarily* be in the present, it is easier and more natural to allow such content to flow freely. In that way your sense of presence remains unfettered.

A common phenomenon in old age is the repetitive recalling of certain incidents from the person's past; and the frequent retelling of them to others often drives younger persons to distraction, and leads to the stereotyping of the elderly as "stuck in the past." Since memories are not pristine or verbatim representations of those incidents, it is more accurate to say that they are *reconstructed* in the present. As Jung (1965) described it in his *Memories*, "Many old people become too involved in their reconstruction of past events . . . [and] . . . they remain imprisoned in these memories." The images harden and the creative potential and enjoyment of them is lost. Jung, of course, allowed the images to flow freely, for he had a truly contemplative old age. The key to the idea of a "time art" in late life is to keep those memory traces, images, and forms at an unfettered and malleable level, so as to enjoy and re-view them creatively in the present. This sort of imaginative creativity applies to much more than memory and the time dimension in later life, as we shall see.

Imaginative Variations

The term *imaginative variation* is used in phenomenology to describe a procedure called the eidetic reduction. The function of the procedure is to reduce the observed mental phenomenon to its essential feature or structure, by imagining all the possible variations on that feature to identify which one remains throughout all the variations. One eliminates the qualities that do not appear in each imagined instance of the phenomenon. The purpose is to classify or categorize the invariable essence of each phenomenon studied, with the same intent as Aristotle had in his categorical classification of things. The difference here, for imaginative aging as distinct from phenomenology, is to allow images to flow freely until one feels or intuits a feature or quality that is *personally* meaningful and aesthetically resonant. The feature does not have to be invariant, for it is ideographic, that is, the resultant image is idiosyncratic and entirely personal, even though it might have broader implications. One then shapes and forms that feature or quality into its most essential or outstanding aesthetic form imaginable.

It has been said that the consolations of imagination are not imaginary, and this is never more so than in later life. When the racing mind slows down and we look with receptive eyes on the myriad images before us, there are all sorts of aesthetic variations available to us. For example, when we wake first thing in the morning, and the mind is still rather fuzzy but receptive and open, we begin to see patterns in the shadows or on the wall or drapery. All sorts of forms and faces, trees and landscapes emerge for us from this receptive mode of seeing and imagining. Leonardo da Vinci reportedly engaged regularly in this sort of process. He would go out and look at a nearby brick wall, which was very worn and weathered, covered with scratches and splotches of discoloration. He would watch it until he began to see a scene or vast panorama on it. On one occasion he started to see a whole battle going on, which became his inspiration for a great mural. Cezanne used to say that this world shows only vacillating, hesitant, and provisional appearances, and he spoke of it as a creation that moans in labor until the artist as its redeemer bestows upon it a final and eternal shape, a proper being. It appears that artists find exceptional success when they have not tried willfully to construct the image entirely by themselves, but, rather, have simply allowed images to emerge.

When it comes to contemplative writing, it is not our task to describe or explain images but to open ourselves to them, and have them affect our thinking and feeling. They have an inherent mystery about them, and that sense of mystery deepens if we develop an attentive attitude toward them in later life. It is not a matter of bettering ourselves by writing about them. There are many books on imaging, urging the purposeful production of images in order to better ourselves, our mental health, our chances of success, and so on. This is not the meaning of imagination *per se*, and it is certainly not all that relevant for the existential realities of old age. At that stage of life, one can enter the mysterious world of dreams and imagination without having to accomplish anything in the outer world. As Schopenhauer (1969) observed, only if we cease to will at all can the object stand out in our consciousness stripped of relations of time, place, cause, and effect.

Images of the past can return to become part of an eternal now, with no need to integrate them along time and space dimensions; we can simply let them be part of the present tapestry of consciousness. Yet this is a moving tapestry, continually being woven anew. Patterns of images may arise from the past, not in clear forms, but in lighter, more ethereal images of persons, places, and experiences, blended into a moving mosaic that is not caught in a static recollection of specific instances. Allowing these partial images and recollections to form, reform, and pass away is a unique aesthetic gift in later life, when one is not required to use these images and recollections for functional purposes, such as for "making it" socially or vocationally. The essence of this art is allowing the memories, images, and experiences of the past form themselves in the present moment in any combination of time, place, or persons, regardless of chronology, sequence, or logic. I use the term "art" here in the same sense as the renowned aesthetician, Benedetto Croce (1965), who claimed that art is not concerned with the true and false, real and unreal, useful or harmful, good or bad, but with an imaginative grasp of the *unique*. For him nothing counts in art but the perfection of the imaginative vision itself, and by its own standard of beauty. If one thinks about it, the essence of this art goes to the heart of the contemplative practice of this book, which essentially consists of allowing, beholding, and letting-go in an ongoing process of appreciation, gratitude, and wonder. Instead of the life-long habit of trying to capture and imprison images in names, categories, or concepts, we let them flow, to form and reform. Images are inherently mysterious, and they invite us to enjoy them well into later life, where mystery deepens the level of our thought and experience.

In this process, there may be images or indistinct impressions that seem to call for expression in words, for they intimate something new, possibly meaningful, or beautiful. The language called for, then, would be figurative and metaphorical, which, of course, is the language of poetry. Many elders may not have the language skills to put these impressions into formal poetry, so they can simply find words to express their impressions in a journal form of contemplative writing. Lacking even this, they can simply appreciate the aesthetic pleasure of the non-verbal process. But one form of poetry that lends itself especially well to this process is Haiku, because of its simplicity and directness. It is much closer in nature to direct apprehension or intuition, and it communicates that without wordiness, interpretive thought, or associative knowledge. Most elders could master it quickly, and they would be expressing themselves in a very ancient and venerable form of poetry. This Japanese verse form is simple: three lines (often preceded by a title), with five syllables in the first line, seven syllables in the second, and five syllables in the third. The other advantage is that the lines do not have to rhyme. Below are a few examples from my own experience, after I had just enjoyed the sheer luxury of allowing an inner state and feeling to emerge and expressed it without prejudgment:

Lassitude

Lassitude abides
At this special time and place
Exquisite pleasure

The "special time and place" this poem expresses is not actual clock time or spatial location, but rather an expression of an eternal present, or Now, which thus suggests something more, perhaps transcendent, than the mere words. Using direct, simple wording can sometimes have intimations going well beyond the words, when they capture a unique personal experience such as the following:

Passing Bird

Passing bird flutters
By my small window—giving
Its benediction

Creatures and objects of nature make particularly good subjects for capturing this spiritual dimension in Haiku. Much like Zen, which prefers a more direct route than the circuitous terminology of philosophy or the wording of more elaborate poetry, Haiku tends to point directly at things. It is experience without ornamentation—a tone, a mood, a transient but sharp sensation of beauty. These are bits and portions of experience, but from them the whole can be envisioned in the brief form of the poem. On this view, the practice of Haiku is a discipline in mindfulness, in which there is attentiveness and recognition of nuances, subtle differences, and resolutions in form and pattern, foreground and background:

Mindful Morning
This mindful morning
Things and thoughts arising—yet
Falling into place

There can also be a sound that evokes recognition and added meaning, such as:

Bullfrog
From across the lake
Throaty, endangered old friend,
Bullfrog croaks anew

So Haiku is a fusion of sensing and feeling, but it is an art form in which all elaboration of ideas and descriptions has been eliminated, so that the sensing/feeling can be immediately and spontaneously experienced. Of course, the simplicity and directness can be captured in other poetic forms; witness Thoreau's delightful little couplet:

The chickadee
Hops near to me

Yet Haiku's simple 5-7-5 syllable form provides a freedom-within-discipline aesthetic experience that is hard to duplicate with other poetic forms. Its directness and immediacy allow us to catch forms and images in flight, in process, which make for a fine written meditation practice in imaginative variations.

As we contemplate the place of creative imagery in conjunction with the stark realities of loss and finitude in later life, we need some sort of aesthetic transition. To accomplish this, we can turn to that master of affective memory, Marcel Proust (1948, p. 221), who wrote,

When nothing remains of our remote past, after the people are dead and the things are destroyed, alone—more fragile yet longer lived, more immaterial, more steadfast, more faithful—the smell and taste of things persist, like souls, ready and waiting to remind us; over the ruin of all the rest they bear unflinchingly on their almost impalpable droplet the immense edifice of memory.

Chapter Seven

Other Dimensions of Being

Imaginative aging takes us into other dimensions of being that can make up a contemplative old age. According to Kant, time and space are the basic dimensions by which we perceive the world. Without these two dimensions, we are incapable of making sense of our experiences, or even our existence. The dimension of time has been the pre-eminent one in the science, philosophy, and literature on the subject of aging, because time is implicit in the very notion of aging. So it will take a bit of imagination to get us out of that dominant dimension and into a consideration of space and the unsung role it has played in contemplative life. Becoming acutely aware of space, placing it more frequently in the foreground and less in the background, is a practice that truly adds a new perspective and dimension to our being in later life. It could be done earlier in life, of course, but most of us are too busy "doing" to give it our attention in being.

Spatiality

Bachelard's *The Poetics of Reverie* (1971), although offering new insights into the qualities and dimensions of reverie, was not as widely influential as his earlier book *The Poetics of Space* (1969), which had a considerable impact on fields such as art, architecture, and literature, as well as philosophy. He had been chair of the department of history and philosophy of science at the Sorbonne from 1940 to 1955, and was internationally known for his writings on the philosophy of science. As a result of his inquiries into Einstein's revolutionary breakthrough in physics and Heisenberg's Uncertainty Principle, there was a marked shift in his focus from physical science to the phenomena of consciousness, from the "axis of objectivization" to that of subjectivity. This led him to an indwelling form of inquiry into the dimension of space. It is a view commensurable with the "In-ness" of Heidegger's (1927) conception of *Dasein*. Being-in-the-world and "in-ness" for Heidegger mean being in a state of mind bound up with both the practical and lived meanings and the value of objects in relation to space. This means not being "in" a geometrically-understood space. For Bachelard, too, inhabited space transcends geometrical space and its abstract, scientifically measurable forms. For him, space is not primarily a container for three-dimensional objects; it is the abode of human consciousness.

Thus, from a purely philosophical point of view, and using a phenomenological approach, Bachelard is led to some conclusions that closely resemble core ideas in the Eastern and Western mystic traditions. One of these is the idea of void, or a pure consciousness without objects, which is the ground of all forms that emerge in our consciousness. Another is the idea of no-mind, or the Unknowing, for in Bachelard's view, the poetic image emerges from a forgetting or not-knowing that "is not ignorance but a difficult transcendence of knowledge . . . which constantly surpasses its origins." Space had this special meaning in the contemplative life of Christian monastics in the Middle Ages, and nowhere was it more tellingly illuminated than in *The Cloud of Unknowing*, written by an anonymous monk in fourteenth century England (Progoff, 1957). The space that this remarkable book elucidates has been referred to as the "mystical space of God." In it, God is present but can only be experienced by "unknowing." It is unknowing because it is empty of all thoughts, things, and images but is still full of God. On this view, the space of contemplation is seen as an empty space or gap between the material world and the eternal world of the spirit. The anonymous monk advises his readers to dwell in that space and remain there until God reaches out for them. Thus, this empty space holds the possibility of being full of God.

There is a very similar spiritual value to space in the Buddhist doctrine of emptiness or the void. Although Buddhism is not a theistic religion, it also claims one has to thoroughly empty the mind in order to experience *sunyata*, a Sanskrit term for "emptiness." Thus it becomes the unconditioned mind, the "unknowing" mind that enables us to experience the unity or the One beyond the world of appearances. At the same time, the emptiness can provide a backdrop or ground from which we can see and experience a broader and richer spectrum of the world before us. We tend to think of space as nothing, devoid of substance or meaning, because of our conditioned minds. Because we tend to think of "real" things as substantive, capable of being measured and weighed, we do not apprehend space as anything at all, except perhaps as a measurable distance between "real" objects. But the reality is that you cannot apprehend a solid without space, nor can you have a figure without a background. Also, we cannot imagine space with no object in it. Nothing but space would be inconceivable and meaningless, because we can only know what we mean through contrast; consequently, objects and space go together like two sides of the same coin. Although space and form go together as the basic things we encounter in this universe, space almost invariably goes unnoticed. To have a more thorough view of the universe in which we live, we need, somehow, to have space become a more prominent feature of our visible world. The aesthetic genius of Chinese and Japanese paintings of nature is the lightness of the brush strokes, which give a slightness and ethereal quality to the *forms* of nature, and thereby enhance the recognition of space and its virtual presence in the whole scene. This sort of vision needs to be incorporated into both our awareness and contemplative practice, as it has much greater outward implications than we might recognize.

Most of us are caught up in things—things to do and things to worry about, to ponder, and even enjoy and gloat over. All of these things are objects and phenomena of our predominant reality, and they continuously throw us off balance. Space awareness, in the midst of our continuous consciousness of these thoughts, feelings, or material objects, can provide us with a whole new perspective. By being aware of space, we are not only aware of objects but also of consciousness itself. Objects no longer dominate, and we can sense a space of stillness in the background while things are present in the foreground. We are almost always not conscious of this space of stillness, this dimension of our being, but it not only frees us from the ego but from the materialistic and mental grip of things upon us. This freedom is the transcendental and spiritual dimension most of us seek. This inner space is a place of profound peace within us that is present even in the face of great distress and pain. It is the peace "which passeth all understanding."

The most direct way to incorporate awareness of this interior space is in meditation, by following the breath into the body and allowing all thoughts to arise and pass away in the spaciousness of our inner awareness. This awareness then becomes a very large space in which to reside. While there, we can open ourselves to the sounds, the sensations, and the spaces between them, including the silence lying within, underneath, and around them. Attending to that space inwardly in meditation attunes us to its presence in the external world as well. Then we are aware of the space that allows everything to be. Paradoxically, by strengthening the perception of space relative to the forms in and around it, we open ourselves to new imaginative ways of apprehending those forms. There is a loosening of the formerly rigid doors of perception created by our lifelong conditioning, and we can more fully engage the aesthetic dimension of imaginative aging discussed in the previous chapter.

Bachelard (1964) calls for attentiveness to the image, but a yielding and allowing attentiveness that opens us to a condition of psychic immensity. He calls this an "intimate immensity of unknowing," and he claims "the simpler the image, the vaster the dream." Beyond the immediate images of intimacy, there are spaces of immensity of depth open to the contemplative mind. He adds that imaginative contemplation can produce an intimate immensity that transports us out of the immediate world to a world that portends infinity. He goes on to claim there is a correspondence between the immensity of world space and the depth of "inner space." The poetic spatiality that moves from deep intimacy to infinite extent in a united expansion was best expressed by Rilke (1984, p. 202), when he said, "Through every human being, unique space, intimate space opens up to the world." For Rilke, it is when human solitude deepens that the two immensities of depth and breadth meet and become identical. We will return later in this chapter to the dimension of solitude, for it is relevant to all the other dimensions of being.

Placefulness

American philosopher Edward Casey (1997, p. 309) has observed, ". . . imagining mind for Bachelard exemplifies a new placefulness, no longer beholden to physical space but acting on its own quasi-autonomous psychical terms. In the imaginal psyche there is no room for anything but places . . . and more places." Placefulness is a dimension of being that is taken for granted throughout most of our lives, yet it is one that offers so much for contemplative aging if it is brought into awareness and experienced more fully and consistently. The reality is that we are embedded in place; it is the ground we stand on, yet it is wherever we go. A current cliché has it that, "wherever you go, there you are." Casey has also observed that we are surrounded by places, we live in places, and we walk over and through them, relate to others in them, and die in them. If you think about it, nothing we do is unplaced.

We are emplaced in the world via our bodies. Whitehead (1929) noted in *Process and Reality* that our presented locus in the material world is defined by some systematic relation to the human body. Spatial existence of a body *in place* is the primary condition of all living perception, not just human. However, our human consciousness and imagination enable us to go beyond the simple location of our body and can take us out of ourselves and into the universe at large. Whitehead (1967, p. 92) makes this concretely clear, as follows:

> You are *in a certain place* perceiving things. Your perception takes place where you are, and is entirely dependent on how your body is functioning. But this functioning of the body *in one place*, exhibits for your cognizance an aspect of the distant environment, fading away into the general knowledge that there are things beyond. If this cognizance conveys knowledge of a transcendent world, it must be because the event which is the bodily life unifies in itself aspects of the universe.

The relativity of one's perspective is so fundamental that we could say the true definition of a person is "a place to look from." This place and its perspective are always unique to the individual because no two persons can occupy precisely the same place at the same time. It is a guarantee of our inviolable individuality. Placefulness and spatiality can be seen conjointly as essential dimensions of our being. With our rational Western penchant for objectifying, for attempting to discern objects within all kinds of contexts, we are usually more aware of location and place than space in each and every context. Although Eastern philosophy and religion pay more attention to space, they are acutely aware of placefulness within space in the material world. Again, Chinese art reflects this beautifully in its landscape paintings. The space that surrounds mountains, mist, and trees renders those figures of nature as essential to the whole picture, but *emplaces* them in a more ethereal and mystic way than most Western paintings.

Bachelard (1971) felt that the image of one's childhood home, especially if it was a warm and nurturing one, is apt to be the most salient one we carry throughout our lives. For elders in general the home is often the single most significant and meaningful place in their reminiscences. The power of place in the human mind has never been made more evident to me than in the remarkable work done by Habib Chaudhury of Simon Fraser University in Vancouver (Chaudhury, 2002; 2005; 2008). He uses personally meaningful visual prompts such as photographs and other mementos from the past homes of elderly residents with dementia, mostly Alzheimer's, in long-term care settings. These prompts, used in interviews with the residents, help to trigger recollections of place-oriented past experiences, which are guided by substantive themes such as "childhood homes," "holding on to emotions," and "emergent present." This "place-therapy" has some exceptional effects on the emotions and cognition of these residents. The cognitive effects are more transient, but the emotional ones lead to uplifting moments of illumination in otherwise unreceptive minds.

As Heidegger (1962) observed in *Being and Time*, from a practical rather than an imaginary point of view, a *place* is not merely a point in a set of abstract grid-like co-ordinates. A place is part of a system or matrix of personal engagements and concerns, and this leads to some strange yet very common phenomena. This became powerfully evident to me when I revisited my childhood home and neighborhood in Buffalo, New York, more than six decades after I had left it. Buffalo had been a vibrant industrial city in my childhood, but it was now a rust-belt city with many demolished and abandoned neighborhoods. Mine had been a lively, multi-ethnic, working class neighborhood in which a Catholic church, school, and churchyard formed the central place for play as well as religious attendance and schooling. When I revisited there decades later, it looked just as it had in my childhood except that it was utterly abandoned. Rather than being vandalized, burned, or razed, it was simply abandoned and left devoid of human existence. The church, the school, the homes, and my grandfather's neighborhood store were there just as they had been, but bereft of life, like an empty Hollywood set. Seeing it like that was a shocking experience, but in a very strange way. It was eerie knowing that the adults who lived in those homes during my childhood were probably all dead, as were many, if not most, of my childhood friends from the neighborhood. The stillness and emptiness were in sharp ıe vitality and noise emanating from that place as I recalled uring my youth.

ıe image of that ghostly neighborhood brought so vividly to e impermanence of things, especially people in places. If the neighborhood had been razed or ruined, the image would have simply been depressing, but the intactness of it made for a much different experience and emotion. I have found myself meditating on that silent place almost daily since the time I revisited it almost two years ago. There was and is a particular kind of sadness to that experience and image, but there was also a certain wistful beauty to it, because it *did* look like I remembered it, and that gave it a feeling of what I can only call transcendent. The reason for describing this personal experience is that it exemplifies a phenomenon called experiential transcendence, which will be more fully developed in the next chapter, but which brings home the power of placefulness here. The concept of experiential transcendence was developed by the noted Yale psychiatrist Robert Jay Lifton (1979, p. 28), who described this unique kind of experience particularly well, as follows: "The feeling is often used to express one's involvement in and, in a sense, passive acceptance of the slow, sad truths of life and nature. . . . the acceptance of and even pleasure in sadness—the sadness of change, loss, and death—has to do with one's sense of being part of the cosmic and the eternal."

Solitude

True contemplation, of course, requires solitude, and there is no more assured place to *be* than in solitude. That said, now is the time to go into the attributes of solitude that are so important for contemplative aging. There is more solitude in later life, and much of it is not by choice. Loss of spouses, partners and other loved ones, family and friends leaves many of us alone in later life. Most elders realize they have to come to terms with this out of necessity, but how much better if one not only accepts this aloneness but begins to reshape it and cultivate it. What begins as loneliness is then transformed into solitude. Although people under fifty-five generally tend to believe that most older people are lonely, elders themselves report that they are seldom lonely (Harris, 1975; Singh & Misra, 2009). Eric Erikson (1986) claimed that many elders relish their time alone so that they can think their own thoughts without distraction, and he felt this is so because ". . . time for solitary reviewing of the past is essential to reconciling the psychological tensions of a lifetime" (p. 141). What else about solitude is there that one can come to relish? For one, the practice of solitude engenders the love of solitude, according to Marcel Proust; and, as Albert Einstein commented in his later years, "I live in that solitude which is painful in youth, but delicious in the years of maturity." In those later years, elders are apt to be more aware that there is stillness and a sanctuary within that you can enter at any time and be yourself. This was attested to by one of the most unlikely elders imaginable, Helen Hayes, first lady of American theater for much of the twentieth century, when she observed: "There were many times in my life, until I was left alone, that I wished for solitude. I now find that I love solitude. I never had the blessed gift of being alone until the last of my loved ones were wrested from me. Now I can go sometimes for days and days without seeing anyone" (O'Brien, 1973, p. 232).

Although never a social butterfly, Thoreau claimed that he never found a companion that was so companionable as solitude. Thoreau is one matter, but most certainly the example of a gregarious celebrity such as Helen Hayes should be a strong argument for the benefits of solitude, and against the charge that it is antisocial or a form of escapism. The contemplative response to this charge is that the direct encounters with self, nature, and the mysterious found in solitude feel more intensely authentic and luminous than most social encounters.

One of the most sublime poets on the subject of solitude was Rainer Maria Rilke, but he took a somewhat different perspective on it when he wrote the following: "And to speak of solitude again, it becomes clearer and clearer that fundamentally this is nothing that one can choose or refrain from. We *are* solitary. We can delude ourselves about this and act as if it were not true. That is all. But how much better it is to recognize that we are alone: yes, even to begin from this realization" (1984, p. 87).

He went on to write about poetic inspiration in his *Letters to a Young Poet*, with the following statement; "What is necessary, after all, is only this: solitude, vast inner solitude. To walk inside yourself and meet no one for hours." And as Bachelard (1964) wrote, ". . . cosmic images are the possessions of the solitary soul which is the principle of all solitude."

We usually think of quiet, stillness, and silence as prime attributes of solitude. Of those, silence is the one that has had the most meaning among creative people who hold solitude in high regard. Emily Dickinson wrote of her "appetite for silence," and Wittgenstein went further, claiming that "only if we enter the zone of silence are we truly human." Wittgenstein was, in his own way, a mystic, and it is notable that mysticism is always directed toward a world beyond speech, a world of silence. Meister Eckhart wrote that God "is the simple ground, the still desert, the simple silence." Taoism, which is often regarded as a mystical philosophy for the spiritual nourishment of the individual, holds silence in the highest regard. This is because, according to the *Tao Te Ching*, existence and the Tao are beyond the power of words to define.

Inborn and Unborn Dimensions

We experience most of our thoughts and feelings about space, time, and place from the perspective of our ego-selves. This is the dimension of our being in which we live almost every minute of our everyday lives, even though we may live in it rather habitually and without a great deal of awareness or insight. We move now into a dimension that is less well known and largely subconscious. It is that innate and "nature" part of the nature/nurture duality discussed in Chapter Three. It is what James Hillman referred to as "that genetic inheritance," the one that is shaped into our unique individual pattern by character in the course of aging. Since this inborn dimension *is* part of nature, the Taoists felt it was wise not to struggle against your inborn nature. Hillman's view is based, of course, on Jung's concept of the archetype, which he described as an *inborn,* unconscious, and pre-existent form that seems to be part of the inherited structure of the psyche. It is instinctual in nature and has no mental content of any sort. Rather, it is an inchoate and primordial image in form, which has no content until it becomes conscious and is filled out with the content of conscious experience. It is closely related to another inborn dimension of being, about which Jung wrote a great deal, *soul.* He claimed that the human soul's universe includes an incredible abundance of images that have accumulated over millions of years of living development and have become fixed in the human organism.

Soul has been defined in different ways by different religions and traditions, and some of them do not distinguish between soul and spirit.

However, it is important to distinguish the material, bodily aspects of soul from the more ethereal definitions of spirit, to be consistent with the contemplative philosophy and practices presented so far in this book. Our bodies live in time and space, governed by the material world, but it is often said that the human spirit lives in eternal truth. Only the soul, it is claimed, has the ability to make connection and establish communication between body and spirit. Spirit, according to this view, refers to the nonmaterial human realm that focuses on eternity, whereas the soul is that nonmaterial realm that is interested in things of the earth. Habitual, unconscious living keeps the eyes of the soul on the outer world, and keeps it hostage to that world by the egocentric demands of the personality. Although grounded in the physical body, the soul can be set free to touch the realm of the spirit in an act of faith, and thereby unite the inner and outer worlds. Soul is also the realm of feeling and image; it is tuned into the realities, positive and negative, of life, and there is much to question, investigate, and discover about its many dimensions. In this sense, it is the lover of art, culture, learning, music, and imagination. These are all conduits of *intuition*, which has been called the voice of the soul, and in an enlivened soul intuition accesses the inspirational realm of the spirit.

Ram Dass has a graphic way of describing the soul in relation to the human ego and the Ground of Being, which he calls "Awareness." He presents a diagram (2000, p. 27) similar to the one in Figure 2 below:

Figure 2

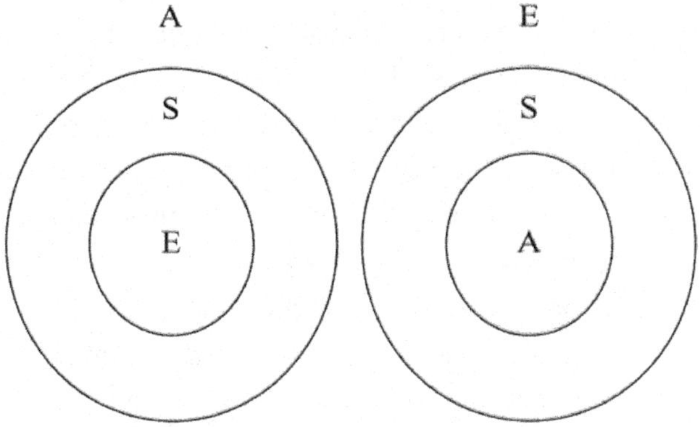

A= Awareness/Ground of Being, **S**= Soul, **E**= Ego

He shows in the left-hand diagram that the ego is a small thing in the sea of Awareness, but, as shown in the right-hand diagram, it is with the ego that we usually approach the world, i.e., "me first." Beyond the ego lies the soul, and he states that "the Soul is here to learn, and aging in all its inevitable difficulties are a prime learning opportunity." As we age we come to learn much about ourselves, the good and the bad; and in the life review stage of development, we learn a great deal about our inborn nature and our past behavior. This is especially so if we have engaged in a truly existential life review. In that process, we drop idealized fantasies of ourselves and confront the shadow side of our personalities. This frees us up to the possibility of honest self-knowledge and self-acceptance, which have been called the very foundation of the soul. By putting soul between ego and Awareness, Ram Dass is taking a position much like that of the fifteenth century philosopher Marselio Ficino, who claimed that we need the soul in the middle to hold together mind and body as well as spirituality and the world.

It can be seen that this inborn dimension is one in which profound psychological and spiritual development can occur, particularly from the vantage point of later life. Soul can be the channel and conduit from ego-dominated being to Enlightenment, or full Awareness, and to touching the Ground of Being. Although not embodied, the soul can be accessed through the inner body via concentration and meditation. In a sense, we have to enter the body to go beyond it. Body-identification is, of course, a basic form of ego, yet it is the one that can be most naturally transcended by inner body awareness and attention. This is done by shifting attention from the external body, with associated thoughts and images of ugliness or loveliness, weakness or strength, of being too fat or too thin, and so on. In old age, of course, beauty fades; the body becomes less attractive and even debilitated, leading to a diminished sense of self-worth and identity. However, an immanent light of consciousness can radiate through the fading form of the weakened body. This is done by attending fully to the feeling of aliveness within, for even the aged body is an alive energy field. In mindful meditation or attention to the breath, one can sense an aliveness that permeates the entire body. This calls for taking your attention deeply into that energy field and becoming one with it. At that level the distinction between inner and outer are dissolved and there is no longer an inner body. In effect, the body itself has been transcended. The "soul work" of this dimension can involve all the contemplative practices discussed in Chapter Five, plus imaginative variations;

for when we are working on archetypal and soul matters, we are dealing with images in our quest for self-discovery. The process of coming to know and engage in the imaginative work of this inborn dimension is like a reunion with something basic to ourselves and has an aesthetic quality to it.

Reuniting with the inborn dimension is a combined physical and spiritual process, whereas connecting with the *unborn* dimension is much more a spiritual process. In several Buddhist schools of thought, the unborn is that which we were before we were born and will be after death. Until there is a realization of our unborn nature, our experience of life will forever be largely dominated by the egoic will to survive, with all its attendant drives and impulses. Seeking this dimension explores a most precious gift, "the great silence of the unborn." This seems somewhat analogous to the realm of the *Cloud of Unknowing*, Meister Eckhart, and other Christian mystics. The Eastern belief is that this is our true nature and it is beyond any of the forms that it can assume. Is this *beyond* being? This is a question worth exploring. However, the greatest impediment to getting in touch with this dimension is our cultural, familial, and educational conditioning. Our feeling and thought processes are so conditioned from the moment of birth, that unburdening ourselves of all that seems like a Promethean task; and conditioning is an even greater impediment to the full awareness of this dimension for the Western mind. Martin Heidegger noted in his later life that Western philosophy has been in great error, because in dichotomizing the intellect, Western humans have been cut off from unity with their own Being and Being itself. He claimed that the error began with Plato, by locating truth in the intellect, which led us to see the world of nature becoming a realm of objects set over against the mind. It is revealing to know that Heidegger came to admire the writings of D. T. Suzuki (Barrett, 1996), the Zen philosopher who was so highly regarded among many philosophers in both the East and West. According to Barrett (1996), Heidegger was reported to have said that, if he understood Suzuki correctly, that is what he had been trying to say in all his writings. As described earlier, in the Buddhist tradition the intent of meditation is to empty the mind of all objects, real and imagined, to achieve no-mindedness. The concept of No-Mind means a mind that is not occupied by thoughts or feelings and is thus open to everything, free of discursive thought and judgment. The doctrine of empti-

f a pure mind empty of all objects and forms, has sometimes been sed with or thought to be equivalent to the Western philosophical notion of nothingness. A Western analytic philosopher would claim that the concept of nothingness (no-thing) is meaningless, for it is object-less and, therefore, non-objective by definition. But from an encompassing perspective, you cannot have a "something" without a "nothing." They are semantically and ideationally conjoined, in the same way you cannot have an "is" without an "isn't."

To get a beautifully descriptive sense of the inborn dimension, we can turn to Admiral Byrd's (1938) account of manning an advanced weather base in the Antarctic during the winter and early spring of 1934. He wrote that, aside from the meteorological work, he wanted to be by himself in complete solitude, because "I wanted something more than just privacy in the geographical sense. I wanted to sink roots into some replenishing philosophy" (p. 9). On April 14, 1934, he made the following entry in his diary (p. 13):

> Took my daily walk at 4 p.m. today . . . I pause to listen to the silence. . . .The day was dying, the night being born—but with great peace. Here were imponderable processes and forces of the cosmos, harmonious and soundless. Harmony, that was it! That was what came out of the silence—a gentle rhythm, the strain of a perfect cord, the music of the spheres, perhaps. It was enough to catch that rhythm, momentarily to be myself a part of it. In that instant I could feel no doubt of man's oneness with the universe. The conviction came that that rhythm was too orderly, too harmonious, too perfect to be a product of blind chance—that, therefore, there must be purpose in the whole and that man was part of that whole and not an accidental off-shoot. It was a feeling that transcended reason; that went to the heart of man's despair and found it groundless. The universe was a cosmos, not a chaos; man was rightfully a part of that cosmos as were the day and night.

It is important to note that Richard Byrd described his family life as an extraordinarily happy one, so he was not escaping from personal unhappiness in seeking the solitude of the Antarctic. He had, however, experienced considerable pressure and anxiety in organizing and trying to fund a number of expeditions for fourteen years prior to his solitary vigil in 1934. He found no time to read the books or listen to the music he wanted to hear. So he was seeking more than privacy in that vigil. Within the silence of the primordial Arctic solitude, he found the "replenishing philosophy" of his quest.

Chapter Eight

Finitude

It is often said that when people, in general, enter the later part of their lives, there is a turn toward greater religious involvement. Folk wisdom has it that it is the awareness of their own mortality, with the fear of both death and the hereafter, that moves older persons toward religion. As one little girl said to her mother, "Grandma reads the bible all the time now. She must be cramming for finals." What are the attitudes of elders toward their own deaths, and do they find religion to be a buffer to the fear of death and dying?

Ultimate Concerns

In his Pulitzer Prize-winning book *The Denial of Death,* Ernest Becker (1973) claimed that death denial is pervasive in human culture, and that anxiety over death is ubiquitous and expresses itself in many different forms. It is not just a question of conscious fear of death as the end of one's life, of finitude, but of the various fears surrounding the event itself. A multidimensional study (Hoelter, 1979) of these fears among the elderly yielded the following: (1) fear of the dying process (including painful or violent deaths); (2) fear of the dead (including avoidance of human or animal bodies); (3) fear of being destroyed (including cremation or dissection of the body for autopsy or organ transplants); (4) fear for significant others (including apprehension about the impact of the respondent's death on others); (5) fear of the unknown (including fear of nonexistence and lack of knowledge about the afterlife); (6) fear of conscious death (including concerns about falsely being declared dead); (7) fear for the body after death (including concerns about decay and isolation of the body); and (8) fear of premature death (concerns about being unable to accomplish desired goals or experiences). Given these and other concerns about the specter of death, it should not be surprising that there are significant differences among older adults in the degree of anxiety, depending on personal disposition, age, illness, religiosity, and other related factors.

Needless to say, people differ from one another in terms of their dispositions or tendency to be anxious in general. We would expect to find that those who are generally prone to anxiety are quite apt to b ious about their personal demise. We are also affected by our expos and death of those around us. The death of loved ones, friends, and even pets can be devastating in its effects on one's emotional well-being and basic sense of security and meaning in the world. How individuals weather these losses will determine to a large extent how well they will handle the prospect of their own deaths. Such losses are an inevitable part of aging and are continual reminders of one's own mortality. For many elders, they give cause to reflect on the meaning of their own lives, since so much of life's meaning was contained in those lost relationships. All this can vary, of course, because for some individuals the loss of their most significant others gives life less meaning and, therefore, less to live for, perhaps making the thought of one's own death less frightful.

Age is certainly a factor. As noted earlier, research has shown that elders are generally less fearful of death than younger age cohorts, and the very old are apt to be the least fearful about death (Cockerell, 2002; Niemeyer & Van Brunt, 1995; Tomer, 2000). Illness, too, can have a major impact on one's attitude toward death. For some, death can be a deliverance from excruciating pain and increasing decrepitude. Illness can also be a harbinger of death, as Florida Scott-Maxwell (1979) describes in her insightful book *The Measure of My Days*. When she was entering her eighties and various chronic illnesses were mounting in her aging body, she wrote, "When a new disability arrives I look about to see if death has come, and I call quietly, 'Death, is that you? Are you there?' So far the disability has answered, 'Don't be silly, it's me'" (p.36).

There is a commonly held belief that religion buffers against the fear of death, but research efforts to demonstrate this have met with mixed results (Duff & Hong, 1995; Fortner & Niemeyer, 1999; Niemeyer, 1994; Wink & Scott, 2005). The broader empirical literature suggests that religious beliefs (e.g., an intrinsic belief in God, belief in an afterlife) are predictive of lower death anxiety (Cicirelli, 2002), whereas religious behaviors (e.g., frequency of church attendance) are not (Wittkowski, 1988). These kinds of findings are due to the differences in what is known as *intrinsic* as opposed to *extrinsic* religious orientation (Cohen et al., 2005; Thorson & Powell, 1990). Extrinsic behaviors consist of things like church attendance and other religious observances for outer rather than inner purposes, such as socializing, maintaining a religious identity and appearance, and following one's received familial religious identification and affiliation, usually without ever seriously exploring the theological basis of the particular religious system. It is utilitarian in nature, serving the need for social status, conformity, and identity.

The American psychologist Gordon Allport was the first to observe these two orientations in his studies of religious belief, whose findings were published in his book *The Individual and His Religion* (1967). Using various types of scales, he found that the extrinsic orientation exhibited less depth and maturity and that it was correlated with racial, religious, and other forms of prejudice. The intrinsic orientation, on the other hand, was correlated with relatively little such prejudice and exhibited greater depth and maturity. The extrinsic believers tend to use their religion in the same way as other social group memberships, and this tends to be exclusionary toward others of a different group or identity. Extrinsic believers also tend to use "petitionary" prayer (e.g., requesting the meeting of tangible needs) rather than "meditative" prayer (e.g., sitting quietly and experiencing the divine). It is not surprising that those who tend to use petitionary prayer tend to use it in dealing with fear of death, which coincides with the incidence of higher death anxiety in extrinsic believers.

It should be pointed out, however, that there are deeply religious people, in the orthodox sense of attending church, praying, and following religious precepts, who are *intrinsic* believers. Intrinsic orientation refers to religiousness that serves as a central framework of faith, meaning, and guidance in life, for example, having a close personal relationship with God and spending time in deep reflection and prayer. These believers show much less evidence of death anxiety than extrinsic believers. It should also be pointed out that, similar to these religious persons, individuals who feel a cosmic-spiritual connection also show less concern about their own death. Recent research by a group of gerontologists (Ai, Park, & Shearer, 2007) finds that having a sacred emotion and sense of reverence in secular contexts had similar positive effects in death preparation. They report that

> these experiences of reverence in secular contexts may reflect an even more intrinsic spirituality . . . which . . . is part of an internalized world view that is truly more integrated into one's

> life. Such a sense of reverence in non-explicitly religious settings may reveal a deeply-held sense of transcendence and positive emotion, perhaps facilitating ability to draw meaning and purpose of life when needed, such as in the face of serious surgery and, perhaps, one's mortality. (Ai, Park & Shearer, 2007, p. 9)

They go on to say that the concept of secular spirituality can be a fruitful research direction in medicine, psychiatry, and other mental health disciplines. They do not mention the concept of gerotranscendence per se, which can apply to religious and non-religious elders alike, but their description of "individuals who felt a spiritual connection with cosmic spiritual entities (e.g., the universe)" sounds much like it. I have found similar instances of "secular spirituality" in my own research and practice, some of which will be reported later in this chapter.

By contrast, those with intrinsic religious beliefs have come to their beliefs by way of serious thought and deep conviction, so that the resulting faith is no longer made up of one's inherited or instilled parental or societal beliefs, but consists of one's personally examined and tested convictions. Subsequent studies using Allport's intrinsic/extrinsic measure have shown that the extrinsic orientation has not only been positively correlated with prejudice and dogmatism, but also with greater fear of death, as noted earlier. From a psychological perspective, all of this suggests that the absence of a well-formulated philosophy of death, whether religious or secular, may be predictive of a greater death anxiety. Perspectives that can serve to reduce the degree of death anxiety are contained in certain images or symbols of continuity in the face of death and finitude.

Symbolic Immortality

When it comes to finitude, we humans often attempt to create, conjure up, and believe in certain images of continuity of self or soul beyond our individual deaths. The noted psychiatrist Robert Jay Lifton (1976, 1979) has spent much of his professional life exploring the place of death in the human imagination. In the process, he has found a human capacity of the symbolizing imagination to deal with the idea of death in terms of a principle of life continuity of the self. That is, we exchange a belief in literal immortality (which we know to be impossible) for a symbolic immortality through "living on" in our children, our children's children, in our works or creations, and in our religions—usually in the form of a hereafter. However, on the basis of his notable studies and clinical work with survivors and witnesses of human annihilation in Hiroshima, in the Holocaust, and of atrocities in the Vietnam War, he has found that these long-standing institutional modes of symbolic immortality are not as viable as they once were for many of us. They certainly were not for many of the survivors he studied and worked with, yet there remained a compelling human need to find sustaining images of continuity among them. Therefore, his major effort was to explore the place of death in the human imagination and how it bears on our sense of endings, changes, and beginnings. He sees the human capacity of the *symbolizing imagination* as enabling us to explore the idea of death and relate it to a principle of life continuity so that we "can know death and transcend it."

On the basis of his studies, Lifton (1979) posited five general modes in which a sense of immortality can be expressed symbolically: (1) the biological, (2) the theological, (3) the creative, (4) the natural, and (5) experiential transcendence. The first and, perhaps, most common mode is the *biological*, which is expressed through family continuity by living on *through* and *in* one's children and their children's children. At a symbolic level, we can imagine an endless chain of such biological attachments after one's death.

Second is the *theological* mode. It is the religious one, in which the basic spiritual principle is the ancient theme of death and rebirth through an immortal soul or spirit. Religiosity and religious beliefs and practices are intended to give one spiritual power over death, which means in a symbolic sense that one is in harmony with a principle extending beyond one's biological time span.

The third form of symbolic immortality is what Lifton called the *creative* mode. This is expressed through the creation of great works of art, literature, or science that outlast the mortal self. This would seem to rule out the majority of us. However, it can be realized through more direct influences on people around us. For example, teachers who never had children of their own can influence generations of students. Physicians, nurses, and psychotherapists can be strongly impelled by an image of therapeutic impact extending through the patient to others, including the patient's children, spouses, and significant others. Charitable and other good works involving human generosity also allow one to "live on" in terms of legacy through the creative mode.

The fourth mode of symbolic immortality is to identify with *nature* itself. This is the belief that nature and the universe around us are timeless and limitless. As a part of them, we live on through all their seasons, changes, and transformations. Within this mode, there is often an image of nurturing and communing with one's own small plot of land, which becomes a metaphor for tending to one's place within the natural scheme of things.

The fifth mode of *experiential transcendence* is of a different order than the other four modes of symbolic immortality, in that death transcendence is "experienced" and not merely imagined or taken on faith. It is a psychic state so intense and all-encompassing that distinctions within time and between life and death disappear. There is a powerful feeling of inner unity, but this level of experience can only be reached by internal contact and confrontation with personal images of life and death that have to be reordered and integrated in what Lifton calls the "formative zone of the psyche." It is also a feeling of oneness in which the self and others, as well as the past, present, future and the universe are merged. This kind of experience is not easily arrived at, especially among people who have survived in the midst of death all around them. The more common experience is a kind of psychic numbing, in which they immunize themselves from the full emotional impact of all they have witnessed, but at the cost of being devitalized and demoralized. This is what Lifton found most commonly among survivors of Hiroshima, for the devastation surrounding them left them with no sense of continuity, including with nature itself. Nevertheless, he found instances of experiential transcendence among some of the survivors; and he was able to help others to achieve some degree of it in his therapeutic work with them, which is discussed shortly below.

There is little doubt that the belief in immortality, whether religious or secular, comes largely from the idea that one's consciousness continues to live on in some form even after the body dies. This idea is ubiquitous and its appeal attests to the supreme subjective value of the life of consciousness, not the life of the body. As Jung (1959, p. 6) wrote, there is a powerful human need to symbolize a consciousness freed from the world as a natural preparation for death, and the idea of the timelessness of the detached consciousness is "in harmony with the religious thought of all times and with that of the overwhelming majority of mankind." The detached consciousness is, in fact, the sense of "being in the world but not of it," which is the goal of all spiritual searching and practice in both Eastern and Western traditions and in mystics the world over.

Along with several other gerontologists, I have looked to Lifton's work in studying variations in death attitudes among the elderly, as reported in both quantitative and qualitative studies of the phenomenon (Hood & Morris, 1983; Sherman, 2008; Vandecreek & Nye, 1993). Questionnaires have been developed by gerontologists in an attempt to determine whether elders do have a preferred mode of symbolic immortality, in line with Lifton's classification. So far, the results have been mixed and without definitive evidence of clear-cut preferences of individuals for one mode of symbolic immortality over the other modes. My own application of such a questionnaire, on a sample of elders ranging from their sixties to their nineties, indicated a great deal of particularity in responses, and a preference for a combination of modes rather than the selection of a single one among the respondents. This called for a study based on direct interviews with individuals, to explore this pattern of combinations of symbolic modes in preference to the selection of one mode. Therefore, I undertook a study involving in-depth interviews with a sub-sample of the survey participants who had various religious and non-religious beliefs and backgrounds (Sherman, 2008).

Early on in the interviews, it became evident that the questionnaire format had not been able to pick up on nuances or delve into the overlapping nature and complexity of the thoughts and images elders have about death and symbolic continuity. To illustrate this, it is best to give actual examples of individuals who were interviewed and compare their questionnaire responses with their more detailed explanations in the interviews. Perhaps the best example to begin with is an elder who identified three modes of symbolic immortality with equally high scores on the questionnaire scales. A brief biography should serve to show how her early and repeated experiences of the deaths of loved ones could lead to overlapping and reinforced feelings and images concerning the subject of death.

She was an attractive but rather pale and fragile-looking woman of seventy-three when I first interviewed her, in a rural hamlet in Upstate New York. She was born and raised in Vermont, in a family of Irish Catholic ancestry on both the maternal and paternal sides. She was the youngest in a family of three girls and four boys, and her oldest sibling, a sister, was seventeen years her senior. Even her youngest sibling, a brother, was seven years older than she was and very protective of her. She had fond positive memories of her early childhood, which she described as "a very, very good one." Her father worked in a pulp mill, but they owned a large old house and a dozen acres in rural Vermont. They were able to grow some crops for sale, but mostly for themselves, and they "never wanted for anything." However, there were many serious illnesses in the family, and most of them proved to be prematurely fatal. Congenital heart conditions seemed to plague the family. Her five oldest siblings died in their forties and fifties. The circumstances of her parents' deaths were particularly tragic in the context of her life. Since the family did not have much money during the Depression, all her brothers and sisters had to quit school and go to work. As the youngest, she was the only one to graduate from high school. Her whole family was looking forward to her graduation, especially her mother and father, but her mother died just before the Christmas preceding her June graduation. Then her father died four months later of a heart attack, or what the family called "a broken heart." Her great regret was that her parents never lived to see her children "because they dearly loved children."

She married the following year, 1941, to a young man whom she had met when she was just a freshman in high school. However, he was inducted into the Army in 1942 and served in the Infantry in the Pacific. Because the Pacific theater of war was particularly bloody, she was in continual fear for her young husband's life during those trying years. He returned home safely and, through the G.I. Bill, they bought some land in Vermont and ran a dairy farm. They had three of their four children there, but he had three heart attacks over the years and had to give up the farming. Then he bought a parking lot in town and managed that until his death. The same pattern of sudden illness and death that had plagued her family of origin plagued her marital family, for her oldest daughter died at age thirty-eight and her own husband died of his fourth heart attack one month later. When asked how she was able to deal with all these osses, she stated emphatically that it was her religious faith. She attended church regularly, including novenas and other observances beyond Sunday attendance. She used the confessional on occasion and took communion regularly. There was no doubt that she had a strong *intrinsic* faith. She had strongly agreed with the following statements on the questionnaire she had filled out: (1) Death is a transition to something even greater than this life; (2) I believe in life after death; and (3) My death does not end my personal existence. According to the questionnaire scales, she had the highest score possible on the *theological* mode of symbolic immortality. However, she scored equally high on the *biological* mode, which consisted of the following statements: (1) My life may end, but that which is important will live on through my family; (2) After death much of myself lives on through my children; and (3) Relationships to family and friends are among the most lasting values. She strongly agreed with all of these statements. When asked if she thought she would see her family again after her own death, she smiled a bit tentatively and said that she did. But she had no idea of what it was going to be like; it was not "a picture in my mind, just a feeling."

The other mode of symbolic immortality she scored high on was *experiential transcendence*. The researchers who designed the questionnaire called it the "*mystical*" mode, probably because of the intimations of cosmic consciousness contained in Lifton's experiential concept and their interpretation of it (Hood & Morris, 1983). Scores on this mode were indicated by degree of agreement or disagreement on the following statements: (1) I have had an experience in which I felt everything in the world to be a part of the same whole; (2) I have had an experience in which I realized the oneness of myself with all things; and (3) I have never had an experience in which I became aware of the unity of all things. It should be noted that this last statement was phrased negatively, so that disagreement with it would be scored positively, in order to avoid response sets that sometimes occur with respondents answering numerous items on a questionnaire. Although this woman scored very high on experiential transcendence, the scale scores cannot give a full indication of the depth of meaning this mode had for her.

Lifton did claim that this mode is characterized by a powerful feeling of inner unity, which these questionnaire statements *do* address. However, he also claimed that it is a psychic state so intense and all-encompassing that distinctions between life and death and within time disappear. Furthermore, this level of experience can only be reached by internal contact and confrontation with personal images of life and death that have to be reordered and integrated, in what he calls the "formative zone of the psyche." These latter points are not addressed in the questionnaire, yet they are an intrinsic part of this woman's actual experience of life and death, including dealing with these realities within the depths of her psyche. In a number of ways, this woman's experience with death in relatively peaceful, rural American settings paralleled that of the people in extreme instances of war and genocide that Lifton studied and worked with. She described vividly her dreams, images, memories, and thoughts about all the loved ones she lost, and how she tried to make sense and meaning of all that in trying to put it into some kind of perspective. She had her Catholic faith and belief in the hereafter, and that helped, but trying to make sense of it here on earth was a different matter. She felt it needed some kind of larger framework, and the idea of the unity of all things and persons made the most sense to her, as she put it, "in a kind of mystical sense." I asked her (as I did at the end of all the interviews I conducted with others) the following question: If you were dying and could choose any image to have in mind, what would it be? Without hesitation she answered "my family." She added that she did not think it was going to be like a reunion, where they all sit down to have a long talk and to catch up on old times. She said, "I think it will be different. I feel, somehow, that there will be no need for that. I will just *be* with them and it will all be fine."

It is significant that the three statements in the *mystical* mode are descriptive of the "cosmic consciousness" component of Tornstam's gerotranscendence theory. It is also significant that those scoring high on that mode showed less death anxiety as a group on the questionnaire scales measuring the fear of death. Although those statements did not fit certain dimensions of Lifton's conception of experiential transcendence, the descriptions given by elders of their high scores involve rich, figurative language and imagery. This is consistent with Lifton's major effort to explore the place of death in the human *imagination* and how it bears on our sense of endings, changes, and beginnings. He felt that the human capacity for "symbolizing imagination" enables us to explore the idea of death and relate it to a principle of life continuity, in which we can know death and yet transcend it. This certainly seemed to be the case in the elders I studied and interviewed, but I was struck by the dramatically different ways in which experiential transcendence occurred in a number of individuals.

A very different combination of symbolic modes from the one just described came from a retired professor who was eighty at the time of our interview. He was a widower, and although he had been married over fifty years, he and his wife never had any children. Not surprisingly, he scored low on the *biological* mode. He was a sociologist by academic training, but he taught for many years in schools of social work at the graduate level. He scored high on the *creative* mode, but that was not so on his initial responses to the following statements concerning that mode on the questionnaire: (1) It is important for me to do something in life for which I will be remembered after I die; (2) If I never do anything significant, my life will have been wasted; and (3) To be creative is to live forever. When it was explained to him that the word "creative" could include activities such as teaching, social service, and so on, he said he would agree more strongly with those statements if he had known this when filling out the questionnaire. He was considered an excellent teacher in reviews by his students, and he felt he was a strong motivator for their desires to be of service as social workers. He also contributed a considerable amount of his savings and assets for student scholarships at two graduate schools in which he had taught. He felt this solidified his legacy, if not his immortality, in his chosen profession.

He was Jewish but not religious, and referred to himself as a "cultural Jew," which was reflected in his low score on the *theological* mode. On the other hand, he scored high on the *natural* mode, which was indicated by agreement or strong agreement with the following statements: (1) Death is as natural as anything else in nature; (2) Only nature is forever, and (3) I may die, but the streams and mountains remain. He added in the interview that as he became older, and especially after his wife developed Alzheimer's Disease, from which she suffered for years before dying, he realized more than ever how much we are a part of nature and that it has its seasons. When asked what image he would want to die by he thought carefully and answered "my wife before the Alzheimer's."

Another individual who scored high on both the *creative* and the *natural* modes was, in fact, a successful artist, sixty-four years old, whose paintings hung in prestigious galleries and museums. He had no problem imagining his paintings being exhibited for generations to come. Since he was a secular Jew, he too was low on the *theological* mode while high on the *natural* mode. Both these men, though secular, mentioned in passing that Judaism does not emphasize an afterlife, and that it was not part of their family or cultural background. Those who identified themselves as atheists or agnostics in the interviews also tended to score high on the *natural* mode. One remarkable example of the *natural* mode as a powerful symbol of immortality was given by a retired Unitarian-Universalist minister who was eighty-three years old when interviewed. What makes it exceptional is that the strong symbolic meaning of nature for him was the result of one experiential transcendence incident, which was different than the cumulative experiences of the woman just described. This man was trained originally as a Universalist minister well before the merger of Unitarians and Universalists in the early 1960s, and his first church assignments were in rural parts of Maine, in the 1940s. Most Universalist parishioners in those places and times accepted New Testament teachings as gospel, usually with the exception of the Trinity. He, on the other hand, was feeling more and more skeptical about the Bible as a source of guidance in his ministry and, therefore, more and more estranged from his rural congregants. Yet he had a memory and an image from his early ministerial training that sustained him beyond the doubts and disillusionments of his later ministry. He described what he called his "epiphany," an event that occurred when he was barely twenty years old, but that has stayed with him, vividly, ever since. He was assigned to a small and remote rural church in Maine as a student minister while in theological school. He was feeling very lonely and lost, not only in that place but in his life at that time. He had not made any real friends at the theological school and he was intensely homesick. The assignment to such a remote church and hamlet only added to his angst. He was living in an upstairs room of a large old house on the outskirts of the hamlet, where he had a room-and-board arrangement as the student minister during the summer. One day, as he looked out the window on the long, treeless field of grass behind the house, he had a most extraordinary experience, which can only be described as transcendent. He was feeling extremely low, but as the summer sun shone on that nondescript field of grass, he had a sudden "overwhelming feeling of ecstasy." He found himself quite lost to any self-consciousness and to time. As he put it, "In that timeless moment life seemed good. Little did I know that life in general, life under that sun, life like unto the grass of the field, that life would seem good, and good from that time forward."

He went on to say that it was an "encompassing experience of exaltation and grace." He felt lost to himself, to any separate consciousness of self, feeling a part of everything—"the field, the sun, and the universe." He has reflected on that memory and that image many, many times over the course of his life, and it sustained him greatly in his future ministries, particularly when he moved to urban churches in the Northeast after the merger of the Unitarian and Universalist Associations in 1961. Unlike the rural congregants of the past, many or most of his new parishioners seemed to be secular humanists, probably agnostic if not atheist. Yet he was able to retain and communicate a strong spirituality in his sermons, as a result of his earlier transcendental experience, and that spirituality appealed to his urban congregations. He explained that, in these later ministries, he relied on William James's definition of religion to guide him. As James (1961, p. 42) put it, "Religion . . . as I now ask you arbitrarily to take it, shall mean for us *the feelings, acts, and experiences of individual men in their solitude, so far as they apprehend themselves to stand in relation to whatever they may consider the divine.*" This retired minister definitely felt that in his youthful solitude, overlooking that field, he had suddenly and unequivocally apprehended himself to stand in direct relation to the divine. He was able to evoke the transcendental experience in his memory and imagination repeatedly over the course of his life. This image and memory replenished his spirit, especially in old age, as he sought more solitude in natural settings similar to the site of his original experience. He never experienced anything like it later in his life, but he did not feel it was necessary to do so, since it was always accessible in his imagination. It was, of course, an exceptional and spontaneous experience that could not be repeated in its pristine entirety. Yet he was able to return to it time and time again when he felt the need of its sustaining image.

It is worth mentioning that this retired minister scored as high on the natural mode as he had on the experiential transcendence one. This would appear understandable in light of the natural setting of his transcendent experience. He was also high on the biological mode, for he and his wife had four married children and numerous grandchildren in whom he could see personal continuity. He had a relatively low score on the theological or religious mode, which seems ironic for a clergyman, but understandable in light of his ministerial experiences and transitions.

Philosophical Finitude

It seems to be the case that those without a belief in an afterlife tend most often to identify with nature as a form of symbolic immortality. In this form, the connecting image of death and life is apt to be the eternal cycle of birth, death, and rebirth. Using this imagery, Jung (1959, p. 6) describes death as "the nourishing soil of the soul. Although there is the unending growth and decay of life, there is a sense of something that lives and endures underneath the eternal flux." Jung called this something the "rhizome." In a similar vein, Lao Tzu said, "Do not fear the aging of the body, for it is the body's way of seeking the root." The "natural" form of symbolic immortality is also achieved through philosophical identification with the whole process of the universe, in which one sees one's own dissolution as part of the natural process of ongoing change.

From a Western perspective, Thomas Mann claimed that the only "religious" way to think of death is as part and parcel of life, and to regard it with the understanding and the emotions to be "the inviolable condition of life." Was this an expression of an intrinsic religious attitude toward death? Perhaps, but it is more clearly a philosophical one. There is an extensive literature on the philosophical attitude toward finitude in Western literature going at least as far back as Plato, who defined philosophy as an exercise for death. Thus, to philosophize is to "practice death." Rainer Maria Rilke (2006), a poet with a deep philosophical bent, claimed that "there is no task as urgent for us as to learn daily how to die." He went so far as to reproach all modern religions for giving their followers nostrums and embellishments of death, "instead of providing them with the means in their soul to accommodate and reach an agreement with it." He went further in exclaiming: "Believe me that death is a *friend*, our most profound friend, maybe the only one who is never, never deterred by our actions or indecision . . . and *this*, you understand, *not* in the sentimental-romantic sense of a denial of life, but our friend especially *then* when we most passionately, most tremblingly affirm our being-here" (Rilke, 2006, p. 112).

This is not far removed from the ancient Greek saying "call no man happy until he is dead." Now this statement can be attributed to a number of things, not the least of which could be the Greek sense of tragedy in life, but the Roman Cicero also claimed that to philosophize is to learn how to die. Perhaps more than any other Western philosopher, Epicurus (1995) had the most forthright approach to finitude when he exclaimed, "Death is nothing to us, since when we are, death has not come, and when death has come, we are not." Death is extinction, pure and simple, no particular problem there.

Walt Whitman had seen the horrific negatives of death in abundance while nursing wounded and dying men in the Civil War. Yet he exclaimed in *Leaves of Grass*, "Let us talk of death—unbosom all freely." He advised that we begin by denying death its greatest advantage, by stripping away its strangeness, engaging with it, having it frequently in mind: "At every instance let us have it before our imagination in all its guises." Lifton (1979), as a first step in his therapeutic approach in working with survivors, called for an "intimacy with death," by looking at it squarely and in all its dimensions. This is not unlike the training of young Buddhist monks, who are required to imagine their own deaths in detail, including burial, rotting flesh, maggots, skeleton, and continued organic disintegration into the earth.

From this organic imagery, we can engage in some more figurative language and venture to say that the body dies because it wants to. When the body is worn out and the brain is tired the whole organism welcomes death. In this vein, Scott-Maxwell (1979) wrote, "Death feels a friend because it will release us from the deterioration of which we cannot see the end." Envisioning this inexorable downward arc, Keats was led to be "half in love with easeful death." Others see death not so much as ending the deterioration of the body as ending the strife and discord of life. Walter Savage Landor, although he wrote sensitive and beautiful poetry, led a contentious life with many public quarrels and litigation. In "The Dying Speech of an Old Philosopher" (1980), which he wrote on his seventy-fifth birthday, he concludes that all of the strife was not worth his while, and ends with "I warm'd both hands before the fire of life/It sinks, and I am ready to depart" (p. 217).

All of this seems to run counter to Sigmund Freud (1958), who used the Greek term *Thanatos* to define the death instinct; and he also used it as a collective name for "all the primitive or instinctual tendencies that lead away from full expression and pleasure toward constriction and toward death." Freud contrasted *Thanatos* with *Eros*, named after the Greek god of love, which he sometimes identified with the constructive impulses or instincts, such as self-preservation, procreation, and especially the sex drive. He proposed that all living creatures have an instinct or impulse to return to the inorganic state from which they emerged. This "drive toward death" is active not only in every creature but in every organism. For example, the metabolic processes active in all cells have both constructive (anabolic) and destructive (catabolic) functions. These processes are opposing, but not adversarial, and work together much like the yin/yang principle. Still, he appeared to give *Thanatos* a somewhat more negative interpretation than *Eros*. Like Ernest Becker (1973), he believed that humans are fearful of death, claiming that all of us in our unconscious do not really believe we will die. The death instinct theory was not fully accepted by therapists, counselors, and educators, even though it had some explanatory value in some cases.

The theory certainly would not have been accepted by Montaigne, who claimed that to practice death is to practice freedom: "Forethought of death is forethought of freedom. Who has learned to die, has unlearned servility. Knowing how to die frees one from all subjection, all constraints." In a similar vein, Epicurus claimed that the consciousness of finitude can give an infinite value to each moment: "Persuade yourself that every new day those dawns will be your last one. And then you will receive each unhoped for hour with gratitude." Schopenhauer called death the "muse of philosophy," and went further to suggest that death itself could be seen as a good thing in its own right. As he stated: "Death is the great opportunity no longer to be I. . . . Dying is the moment of that liberation from the one-sidedness of an individuality which does not constitute the innermost kernel of our true being, but is rather to be thought of as a kind of aberration thereof" (1969, pp. 507-508).

What Schopenhauer meant by this was that the I, the individual I am, is merely a part of the world of phenomena, but if I am also something in myself which is outside of the world of time and change, then death might not be my absolute end, my finitude. He was making use of

Kant's distinction between the thing-in-itself and a mere phenomenon. The *Ding-an-sich* (thing-in-itself) is not available to our senses or intellect so we cannot know things in themselves, the *noumena*, but only their appearances as *phenomena*, and these are only *representations* of the *real* things in themselves. So bodies, like ours, together with the space they occupy, must be nothing more than representations in us that can exist nowhere else than in our thought and imagination. On the other hand, the realities of the thing-in-itself are eternal and not subject to any kind of individuation; thus the individual I is an ephemeral phenomenon.

How can this idea be consoling in a practical sense, for example, in contemplative practice? To think of it imaginatively is one possibility. What we mean by the individual I is an image of ourselves. It is what you think about yourself and what you imagine yourself to be, along with all that your friends, relatives, and others have told you about yourself. Consequently, this image of yourself is not the real you any more than your photograph is you. No image of *anything* is *it*, the thing in itself. So when Schopenhauer says that our individual I is not "the innermost kernel of our true being," he means that the center of the self needs to be located at a deeper and more universal level than we are accustomed to in our culture. This is indicative of the fact that Schopenhauer was much influenced by Buddhist thought and, therefore, viewed the extinction of the phenomenal I as an entrance into *Nirvana*. This is a rather optimistic view of death for such a renowned pessimist as Schopenhauer. On the other hand, the first of the Four Noble Truths of Buddhism is that all existence is filled with suffering, and Schopenhauer went so far as to claim that "constant suffering is essential to all life." So his pessimism about life helps to explain his rather positive view of death.

Although we can say metaphorically that in very old age the body might "welcome" death, ironically no one is permitted to die of "old age" in our society. It is not a medically acceptable diagnostic category. Yet if we were more sensitive to and expressive of the feelings and impulses of the whole organism, we would, like the ancient Greeks, view death more positively as a release. Although they worshiped the body in their culture and art, especially the beautiful bodies of youth, the venerable Greeks were also profoundly philosophical. They recognized that if one abides philosophically and sensitively in the natural, gradual dissolution of the body over a lifetime, it can lead to a comprehensive and more positive view of the arrival of death. On this view, death is not the opposite of life, as is commonly thought; the opposite of death is birth, but life is eternal. This can be seen as a form of philosophical understanding and faith in the whole process of life and death, of being and non-being alike.

Chapter Nine

Beyond Being?

Having just explored *symbolic* immortality, the title of this chapter might suggest that it will be an exploration of *real* immortality. That would not be a realistic task. It is something human beings have been pondering and exploring since the dawn of human consciousness and the realization of our personal finitude. The research on the various forms of symbolic immortality, after all, was explored in order to see what it could tell us about the fear of death among the elderly, and how that compares with younger age groups. Even though there is a great deal of variability in fear of death and finitude among individual elders, it is now clear that they are generally less fearful of death than younger age cohorts. This is very consistent with the theory of gerotranscendence, which holds that a decreased fear of death is a natural psychological development in old age. The theory was introduced early in this book because it suggests some promising ontological developments in later life, which speak to the subtitle of the book, "A Way of Being in Later Life." What needs to be explored in this chapter is the "transcendence" part of gerotranscendence. The term transcendence denotes going *beyond* or surpassing. So just what is transcended in later life? Does the theory speak to that question and to what extent?

Gerotranscendence Revisited

Lars Tornstam, who developed the theory, explains his meaning of transcendence by posing a hypothetical comparison of a Western elder with a Zen Buddhist. As a result of the process of aging, a different mind-set or meta-perspective emerges in the elder that is similar to a Zen perspective. Tornstam (2005, p. 38) states that the Zen Buddhist "would call himself *transcendent* in the sense that he lives in another, more boundary-free world compared with most of us in Western societies." He goes on to suggest that in the process of living and aging, the degree of transcendence increases from young adulthood into old age. This process toward *gero*-transcendence is intrinsic and culture-free, generated by normal living, though it can be modified by certain cultural patterns. If this process is not impeded by psychological or cultural elements, it can lead to an enlightened maturity and shift in meta-perspective, from a materialistic and rationalistic world-view toward a more cosmic and transcendent one. This includes an increasing feeling of cosmic communion with the spirit of the universe, though it is not in the form of some figurative sort of sky-gazing, but rather in an increasing interest in the small, everyday experiences in life and nature. Tornstam explains this as follows: "The experience of nature evokes the feeling of being at one with the universe, which is called *at-one-moment* in the Eastern tradition. The increasing significance of these small everyday experiences of nature could therefore be interpreted as a way in which the barrier between the self and the universe is transcended" (2005, pp. 59-60). Along with this is the development of a sense of mystery about many things that have been taken for granted, as mundane, routine, and meaningless. The theory also holds that there is an increased amount of time spent in "meditation," not usually in formal meditative practice but in a more contemplative frame of mind. This goes hand-in-hand with a preference for more solitude than in younger years.

Another development is a redefinition of the perception of time, space, and objects, some of which was described in earlier chapters of this book. This involves a redefinition away from linear and deterministic conceptions of time to more flexible and interactive conceptions of past, present, and future. In addition to a decreased fear of death, the theory holds that there is an increased blurring of the boundaries between life and death. There is a correspondingly decreased interest in material things, as well as a decreased interest in superfluous social interaction. This does not mean the person becomes more self-preoccupied, for in fact there is a *decrease* in self-centeredness. Tornstam describes this as a form of self-transcendence. So in the words of Emily Dickinson, the self-transcended elder can cheerfully exclaim, "I'm nobody! Who are you?" and feel quite good about it.

There has been further testing of this theory since the initial presentation of its formulation, and test results presented in professional publications in this country rather than in Sweden, where the theory originated and was tested and formulated in the 1980s. In one of these later studies, the American researchers used a series of focus groups in the United States to refine and revise the original gerotranscendence scale (Atchley, 2009).The analysis of the data from their study indicated that the core measure of gerotranscendence revolved around three items from the scale: (1) feeling a greater connection to the universe, (2) finding greater satisfaction from one's inner life, and (3) having less fear of death.

Over the past decade, a number of representative studies of older populations have tested the gerotranscendence scale, and in those studies the cosmic transcendence element of the scale has emerged as particularly consistent. A 2006 study of 928 older Dutch adults examined the relationship of this element to having a framework of meaning in life, and whether religiousness and demographic characteristics were involved in the relationship (Braam, Bramsen, van Tilburg, van der Ploed, & Deeg, 2006). The results showed a substantial, positive relationship between the cosmic transcendence element and a scale that measures the extent to which one has a framework and philosophy that gives significant meaning to one's life. The relationship was much more pronounced among those who were *less* involved in religions, women, age seventy-five or older, and widowed. The study also cautioned that the personal relevance of cosmic transcendence depends on cultural factors, such as the secularization of the society in which the elders live.

There are several interesting aspects to the findings of this study, but foremost is the fact that it was those who were *less* involved in religion who showed the strongest association between cosmic consciousness and having a significant sense of meaning in their lives. One might speculate that since religious involvement provides a *prescribed* sense of meaning in life, it could be that, if one is secular and not religiously involved, then one might have to look more intensely and independently for a sense of meaning in life. Yet one has to be aware that the Netherlands, Denmark, and Sweden, where much of the gerotranscendence research has taken place, are more secular societies than the United States, where over eighty per cent of adults claim to be religious and over ninety per cent believe in God. Still, the same dynamic could be operative among secular elders in this country, regardless of its ostensibly greater religiosity. My own survey research and phenomenological study of that subject suggests that this *is* the case. One consistent finding in all these studies is that those with high scores on gerotranscendence show high scores on life satisfaction. In short, gerotranscendence appears to make for higher morale in *this* life. Another finding of significance in several of the studies is a feature of gerotranscendence they call "everyday wisdom," which is marked by a reluctance to make quick or absolute judgments of right and wrong. Thus, there is evidence of an increased broad-mindedness and tolerance as well as transcendence of the right/wrong duality characteristic of a less mature morality. This runs counter to the popular stereotype of the older person as having a more rigid and calcified mind-set.

The findings concerning cosmic consciousness in the gerotranscendence studies and those concerning the experiential transcendence mode of symbolic immortality call for closer scrutiny. They are both, after all, attempting to describe forms of transcendence that have a strong bearing on the ontology of later life. For example, statements from the gerotranscendence questionnaires such as "I feel connected with the entire universe" and "I feel that I am part of everything alive," and statements from the symbolic immortality questionnaire such as "I have had an experience in which I realized the oneness of myself with all things" and "I have had an experience in which I felt everything in the world to be part of the same whole," have considerable similarity. The key difference is that the two experiential transcendence statements include the word "experience," which attempts to find out if the person has had a direct experience of transcendence. To "feel" that one is connected to the entire universe or part of everything alive can be the result of a general feeling or belief rather than based on an actual experiential event or events that involve perceptual loss of personal boundaries in a larger cosmic sense. There is undoubtedly some overlap in the two indicators of transcendence, in that some individuals having high gerotranscendence scores have, in fact, had such transcendental experiences. There is also a strong possibility that many of those who score high on gerotranscendence have not had such experiences, but instead have *developed* the cosmic meta-perspective or world-view through the natural process of aging, as the theory proposes. This is not to say that this meta-perspective is lacking in transcendental value. On the contrary, the empirical results show that it *has* such value, and that is why it is so relevant to the central thrust of this book. Having such a meta-perspective in later life has inherent value, regardless of whether or not the person has had transcendental experiences as described by Lifton (1979). The reason this comparison is being made is that elements of both gerotranscendence and experiential transcendence might complement and strengthen one another in ways that allow us to speak about a process of experiential *enlightenment* that can take place in later life.

Experiential Enlightenment

The first point that has to be made here is that experiential transcendence is just one of five modes of symbolic immortality in a general theory of death transcendence. Gerotranscendence, on the other hand, is a general theory in its own right, so in one sense we will be looking at what experiential transcendence can add to that general theory. Both forms of transcendence lead to a reduced fear of death, but gerotranscendence accounts for considerably more developments in the aging process than just that. However, it is significant that both Tornstam and Lifton turn to the Eastern philosophy of Zen in describing and developing some key features of their respective theories. Tornstam's hypothetical comparison of the gerotranscendent and Zen meta-perspectives has already been described. Lifton, in his book *The Broken Connection* (1979), calls attention to the fact that Japanese culture in the Zen tradition has for centuries emphasized forms of experiential transcendence in its spiritual and physical disciplines. Without going into specific detail, Zen is a school of Mahayana Buddhism that emphasizes "experiential wisdom," which downplays cerebral knowledge and the study of religious texts in favor of direct, experiential enlightenment through meditation, self-contemplation, and intuition. Zen is referred to simply as "the path of enlightenment." The choice of "experiential enlightenment" as the title for this section of the chapter should become more evident as we proceed. For example, in the appendix of his book *Gerotranscendence*, Tornstam (2005, p. 197) suggests the following exercise, called "Being a Flower," to enhance personal development in later life:

> Go outdoors and find a beautiful flower of your liking. Concentrate on that flower and contemplate the fact that you and this flower are made of the very same basic molecular components. Try to comprehend that by this fact the flower is part of you, and you are part of the flower, at the same time as both you and flower are parts of the universe. Try to feel how the separateness of you and the flower is transcended and substituted with a feeling of wholeness and togetherness. You and the flower are

the same. Experience the joy and pleasure of this comprehension.

This exercise apparently has the intention of eliciting a Zen-like experience and evoking a more direct experience of cosmic consciousness through imagery. This is the chief ingredient that Lifton's experiential transcendence can bring to the more general theory of gerotranscendence. And all of this, of course, is in the service of enlightenment. However, it should be noted that Tornstam does not ignore direct experience as an initiator of transcendence. Life crises, such as the death of a beloved spouse, can lead to transcendence, even though the immediate impact may be experienced as devastating. In effect, the surviving spouse has learned directly and powerfully the transience of people and things in life, and has gained a deeper *acceptance* of that fact. Acceptance of impermanence is an essential feature of enlightenment in Eastern traditions.

The power of experiential transcendence cannot be minimized. It depends entirely on a psychic state so intense and all-encompassing that even time and death disappear from consciousness. There are mystical characteristics to this psychic state, ineffability and, at the same time, immediacy and experiential validation of something vital. Such experiences lend certitude about that something, which the persons do not just believe on faith, but that they now *know* because they have experienced or "had witness" to it. Lifton calls this "the classical mode of the mystic." An example of this is the eighty-six year old minister quoted in Chapter Eight, who had the epiphany in which he felt an "overwhelming feeling of ecstasy" as he looked over a long field of grass. It should be recalled that this was a liberal, Unitarian-Universalist minister who even in the theological school had grave doubts about the existence of God, and remained agnostic throughout his life. Yet, he had a transcendent experience that was linked to an image and an actuality in nature. He had always been an admirer of the Transcendentalists, especially Emerson and Thoreau, who saw the spiritual in nature, so we could reasonably assume he would have developed his gerotranscendence in the process of aging without having experienced his epiphany. However, as a result of that experience, he had no doubt that this was, indeed, a transcendent event of cosmic consciousness. As reported earlier, he never had such an experience again, but that was not necessary: As Lifton (1979, p. 26) states, "One never 'returns' to exactly the same inner structure of the self. Having once broken old forms, one senses that they can be broken again, or at least extended beyond earlier limitations. In addition, an important memory remains a still active image-feeling of intense inner unity." From this kind of experience can come an overriding visualized image, which in Sanskrit is called *ishtadeva,* and which becomes the chosen ideal or guiding divinity of our contemplation. Even if our *ishtadeva* is not represented in a single image, it can be made present by visualizing associated symbolic forms, such as revered persons, places of pilgrimage, or of natural beauty and meaning. It was evident to me from in-depth interviews with certain elders that they had gone through such a process, in conjunction with at least one "mystical" experience or instance of experiential transcendence. For those who had experienced this and incorporated it with images or meanings from other sources, it was always accessible when needed, and it was always available for contemplation. Bernard Berenson (1949, p. 18) referred to these experiences as moments of "perfect harmony," and wrote of one such moment as follows: "It was a morning in early summer. A silver haze shimmered and trembled over the lime trees. The air was laden with their fragrance. The temperature was like a caress. I remember—I need not recall—that I climbed up a tree stump and felt suddenly immersed in Itness. I did not call it by that name. I had no need for words. It and I were one."

A New Being?

Paul Tillich's (1952) concept of the *Ground of Being* offered a provocative alternative to the conventional anthropomorphic conception of God, and it contributed to a rich existentialist discourse on being, following World War II. He later introduced a related idea in a treatise called *The New Being* (1955). As an existentialist, he saw the need to confront our basic anxiety in order to have the "courage to be." This anxiety, at its base, is much as it was described by Sartre in *Nausea*—an abhorrence of one's self, a nauseous disgust with it, because one sees one's self as the opposite of an idealized image of what one *should* be. Tillich claimed that if we call up the courage to take on upon ourselves our own anxiety, we have the astonishing experience of feeling reunited with the self. This is not done in false pride and self-satisfaction, but rather in a deep self-acceptance, in which one accepts one's faults, flaws, virtues, and vices, but in the process one discovers one's existential significance and meaning. The self-hatred and disgust disappear, and there is a center, a meaning, and a direction for life. "All healing—bodily and mental—creates this reunion of one's self with one's self. Where there is real healing, *there* is the New Being" (Tillich, 1955, p. 22).

Elders who have gone through what was mentioned earlier as an existential life review have had to confront actions, behaviors, and hatreds of theirs from their personal pasts, which they have been deeply ashamed of and have very much regretted. Such a review can stir the profound existential anxiety of which Tillich speaks. It can be extremely demoralizing and depressing, yet most elders who go through it emerge with a sense of healing and a reunion with the self. But if this is a *reunion* with one's self, is this really a *new* being? According to Tillich, it *is* a new sense of being and it appears as a form of grace. This spiritual grace originates, according to him, from the Divine Ground of All Being, and it is given for the purpose of helping us to achieve our final end, which is to return out of time and the ego-self to that Ground. It is a natural kind of grace, in that it is derived from a source having nothing at all to do with who we are or what we have done in this life; it is totally other, not an earned grace but a true grace without restriction. This is alien to our conditioned ego-selves, which are instilled with the imperative that grace has to be earned through our egoistic efforts.

In this regard, the problem with the ego-self is its imperious sense of mind over matter, of a mind that can control all the organismic impulses, directions, and aspirations of the person. It is the hubris of this ego consciousness that is responsible for the idealized image of what we *should* be like but never are, and makes for the shame and regrets we experience in life, especially in old age. A major feature of this hubris is a belief in the mind having power over one's body, which results in a duality of mind and body, and an internal struggle in which there is never a feeling of organic wholeness or oneness. Contemplative traditions emphasize in words and practice the intimate and inseparable relationship between mind and body, and include exercises that enable the person to overcome the duality and experience the unity of an embodied mind. Mindfulness meditation that focuses attention on the breath enables the person to experience the breath and the mind as one and the same. The marvelous feature of the breath is that it can be both voluntary and involuntary at one and the same time. Breath occurs naturally without our willing it, and we would not survive if it did not do so, but we can consciously allow it to be long or short, deep or shallow, and so on. The breath breathes us as we breathe it, in an experiential nexus where we are both subject and object simultaneously. It is an unusual and strangely liberating experience that can be had repeatedly in mindfulness meditation.

This experience fits well with the doctrine of interdependent arising, which holds that the whole phenomenal world comes into being altogether, and that the apparent "things" in the world are all dependent on one another. This is experienced most immediately and intimately in that nexus of willing/non-willing while mindfully meditating on the breath. In this state, we feel both determined and determining, a most unusual and strangely reassuring experience. This sense of interdependence or interbeing of all things, if one is regularly attentive to it, can lead to a remarkable feeling of rightness or "thusness" about most things and happenings. Everything is taken as "such-as-it-is," and feels as though it could not be other than what it is. This is consistent with a teaching of Buddhist philosophy, that nothing would be as it is without this fundamental reality or "thusness," called, *tahata*. It is the "suchness" of things, of viewing them as they are. "It is an affirmation through and through. I see a tree, and I state that it is a tree; I hear a bird sing and I say that a bird sings; a spade is a spade; and a mountain is a mountain; the fowls of the air fly by and the flowers of the field bloom: these are statements of *tathata*" (Suzuki, 1956, p. 263). As clear as objects such as birds and mountains are to our eyes and minds, the "thusness" of things implies something more profound, indescribable, mystical, and can only be indicated as "thus," "in such manner," or "such-as-it-is." The object or thing is only the appearance of an underlying ultimate reality. Yet this insight yields a general feeling that each thing, thought, image, emotion, and so on, is exactly as it should be—authentic, complete, and utterly appropriate, "such as it is."

It becomes apparent that life is sufficiently miraculous already, but *we do not notice* it in our everyday consciousness. If we catch a glimpse of its mystery, its "thusness," we momentarily experience new emotions and thoughts, but these come from within as a passing insight or, perhaps, as an awakening of the spirit. What is needed for a new being in later life is recognition that the spiritual is not to be separated from the material, particularly the body, nor the ordinary from the wonderful.

Mindfully attending to the ordinary can lead to extraordinary delight and wonder, to the realization that everything is just right as it is and as it can ever be. What sometimes happens in the course of this mindful attending is a sudden cosmic clarity of the truth of this. Unfortunately there is an arcane and even occult connotation to the term "cosmic," to suggest that it is other-worldly and can only happen to exceptional people at exceptional times. Yet it can and does occur in unremarkable people in unremarkable times and places. It comes as an insight and illumination that the universe and everything in it are so utterly *right* exactly as they are, in that moment, that there is no need to try to explain or validate the insight. It can be concretely physical and material in its manifestation, yet perhaps for this very reason it seems ineffable and indescribable in any concretely descriptive terms. The idea of cosmic consciousness has been viewed and used in various ways by different thinkers and traditions, but since it is used in the theory of gerotranscendence, and since our concern is with contemplative experience in later life, it would be helpful to look at these different uses of the term. Each one of them elicits its own imagery and figurative language, so it behooves us to try to find the commonalities beneath these differences. Furthermore, exploring the imagery and language of each of these might be suggestive for contemplative practice in our place and time.

There was one ancient conception of cosmic consciousness in the West, among the Greeks, which paralleled similar ideas in the East for centuries. The pre-Socratic Greeks saw no distinction between spirit or mind and matter; and in the case of Anaximander, the universe was conceived of as an organic whole supported by a cosmic breath, the *pneuma*, which also sustains the human body. A primary feature of this way of thinking was the emphasis on change and flux. Heraclitus epitomized this view. He held that we live in a universe of perpetual change, a continuous flow and change of all things, as famously captured in his expression, "You could not step twice into the same river, for other waters are ever floating on to you." He saw also that all changes arise from the cyclic and dynamic interplay of opposites, and yet he claimed that these opposites form a final unity. The ultimate unity that transcends all these opposing forces he called the *Logos*. Modern relativity theory has demonstrated that mass is not any substance, but a form of energy, and that the whole universe appears to be a dynamic web of inseparable energy patterns. This emphasis on dynamic change and interaction is thus common to both the ancient Greek and modern scientific views. If we look at the individual within this view, it is as though the person is a locus of energy in a cosmic energy field or pattern. It provides a very suggestive and dynamic kind of imagery, and it is interesting that ancient meditative practices and exercises saw the body as such a locus.

The ancient Chinese used the word *chi* (as do many modern Chinese) to describe the energy that animates the cosmos and the human body, the latter through various pathways, as described in traditional Chinese medicine. The yin/yang concept of ancient Chinese philosophy is strikingly like that of Heraclitus and his conception of the dynamic unity of opposites. Interestingly, breath is central to the ancient Chinese exercises known as *Qigong*, in which the breath attunes one to the energy or *chi* that vitalizes the various parts and organs of the body. For Heraclitus, breathing not only brings in oxygen, which is transformed into life-giving energy for the body, but it also brings knowledge with it. We take in knowledge coming from the *Logos* when we inhale, and we surrender to its truth as we exhale. This is not unlike the process, both mental and physical, in mindfulness meditation. Breath is knowledge in this metaphorical sense, and breath exercises and imagery can elicit a sense of cosmic connectedness. Although there is flux and flow all around, there is a deep knowing or intelligence within the eye of the storm, as it were. In fact, Heraclitus held that *Logos* is a transcendent intelligence that organizes the discrete and ever-changing elements of the world into a coherent whole.

This recognition of the flux and flow of our earthly existence and the wisdom of tuning into its rhythms, vagaries, and patterns within our bodies and our environment is characteristic not only of ancient Greeks, like Heraclitus, but also of ancient Chinese Taoists, like Lao Tzu and Chuang Tzu. This path to spirituality or the divine celebrates the earth, the body, and their manifestations. It may even identify the Spirit with the sensory world or, like Spinoza, make no distinction between mind and matter in God's universe. The divine is immanent in everything throughout the perceptible natural world. Thus, it is a pluralistic view of the universe and of human existence, and its primary perspective is of the many rather than the one. William James (1996) epitomizes this view in his treatise on "a pluralistic universe," which stands in the tradition of

Heraclitus on both this and the process/change view of reality. This is the way of immanence in approaching the divine, and can be contrasted with the "ascendant" way, which is transcendent in being above the physical manifestation of this earthly world and existence. The ascendant glorifies heaven, not earth, and the One, not the Many. In the West, this ascending and otherworldly tradition was largely Christian and held sway up to the time of Copernicus, but there were elements of it among the ancient Greeks and even in Buddhist and Hindu traditions from the East. It aims at a consciousness that is ethereal and beyond the body and the earth, though it is aware of them. It also aims to get rid of an earthly self by disidentifying with the ego, with the body, or with any other object. It aspires to a pure consciousness and points to a void or emptiness as the undifferentiated reality underlying all apparent things, perhaps the One. For the ancient Plotinus, everything that exists emerges from the One in an eternal process of emanation, and everything and everyone aspires to return to the One. He felt that the essential person outgrows being and becomes identified with transcendence into the One. On this view, such transcendence would indeed be "beyond being." But most of us are probably not capable of achieving such a state of pure consciousness, of "no-thing" or emptiness, even with deep and lengthy meditation. Even among devoted meditators, from different meditative schools or traditions, there is strong disagreement about whether an absolutely pure consciousness can be attained through meditation, prayer, or related disciplines in our earthly existence (Katz, 1990).

Even Heraclitus, who emphasized change and flux and the Many rather than the One, felt that everything emanated from and ultimately returned to the *Logos*. Although he conceived the world as strife and tension between opposite forces, this tension could finally be represented as a harmony in the *Logos*, much like the yin/yang in the *Tao*. The *Tao* can be seen as the transcendent source of all things, and while determinate things change, the *Tao* itself does not. Even William James (1956), who also emphasized change and flux and the Many rather than the One in his pluralism, felt that there was an encompassing consciousness, a "mother sea," into which all the individuality and dynamics of the Many flow, as into a reservoir. The one common feature of both the ascending and immanent routes is that they take us out of our ego selves, out of the false sense of "I" that distorts reality, because it is based on a duality of an I or ego that feels it is independent of and can be in control of its body and environment, when in fact it is alienated from both. In other words, our ordinary feeling of I causes us to understand many things wrongly. It has been well said that "We do not see things as *they* are but as *we* are." Perhaps this accounts for the ancient Indian notion that manifest being is somehow illusory, and that the way in which we experience the world disguises the true unity of the world. It is not necessary to think that appearances are themselves illusions, but rather that they show us only the part of reality that is conditioned by our upbringing, culture, and personal life experiences. However, a diligent inward mindfulness can free us from the illusory preconceptions and prior scripting of our minds, so as to view inner and outer appearances with calm detachment and openness. In this sense, inner reality is primary and outer reality is secondary. It is primary from a transcendental as well as an immanent point of view, for it is the primary reality of the soul. As Eckhart said, all the liberating inner truth and vision we need, other than the practical knowledge of empirical things, is "native within us." It needs to be realized first from within, even though it ultimately transcends inner and outer, encompassing all.

The Present and the Perennial

Staying in the present rather than straying into the past and future is a very difficult state of consciousness to maintain. William James' concept of the stream of consciousness is very consistent with our actual experience. Consciousness flows with all its flotsam and jetsam of memories, images, thoughts, feelings, anticipations, and shards of all sorts of mental detritus. Much of the problem in maintaining *presence* is self-consciousness, or ego-consciousness, which is essentially a bondage to time through a complex of memories and anticipations. Yet because the present is an infinitesimal point without size, there is no room for the ego in it. If the ego could be released from the time-space frame in which it is bound, there would be a recognition that underlying memory, anticipation, and all the other phenomena there is a center of unmoving consciousness that never, at any point, departs from present reality.

A lot of popular attention is currently being given to the concept of "the power of now" in New Age publications and presentations, and this is all to the good, for the *Now* has a long and venerable history, in Eastern as well as in Western philosophy. Both the Epicureans and the Stoics valued the present above the past and, even more, the future. It was axiomatic for them that happiness can only be found in the present, and that one instant of happiness is equivalent to an eternity of happiness. It can always be found immediately, here and now. They wanted to re-situate the present moment within the perspective of the cosmos, and thereby accord infinite value to that fleeting moment of existence in the now. Later, near the end of the Enlightenment, Jean-Jacques Rousseau (1979), in his *Reveries of the Solitary Walker*, waxed poetic about the glory of being in the present. Focusing on the present, he stated, brings on the simple "sensation of existence," which is the sensation of being *in* the whole and the sensation of the existence *of* the whole. For him, it was a passive and almost mystical experience not requiring effort, which was unlike the Stoics and Epicureans, who had exercises to separate oneself from the past and future and delimit oneself to the present moment. While Rousseau waxed poetic, the poet William Blake exclaimed "I see the Past, Present, and Future existing all at once before me." Blake was a visionary not only as an artist and poet; he also brought a sense of something greater into every moment of life, lending a sanctity and wholeness to the present that intimates an eternal *now*.

Paul Tillich (1963), in *The Eternal Now*, states that "the riddle of the present is the deepest of all the riddles of time," because there is no "present" if we think of the never-ending flux of time. He observes that the mystery of the future and the mystery of the past are united in the mystery of the present. If we accept the present, not caring that it is gone in the moment that we accept it, we live in it and it is renewed for us in every new "present." In the words of the ancient Hebrews, we live so long as it is still today. People who are never aware of this experience lose the possibility of resting in the present, or as the Hebrews described it, they never enter into "divine rest." They are held back by the past or escape into the future, not able to rest in the present and enter the eternal rest, which stops the flux of time and gives us the blessing of time. Philo claimed that "today" means boundless and inexhaustible eternity, and that periods of months and years, and time in general, are ideas of those who calculate by numbers, but the true name of eternity is "today."

Not everyone, and no one all the time, is aware of this "eternal now" within the temporal now. Yet it does from time to time break into our consciousness and give us the certainty of the eternal in the now; for eternity is timelessness rather than never-ending time, and is thus present at every point in time. Emerson (1981) lamented that we postpone or remember rather than living in the present. We are heedless of the riches surrounding us as we stand "on tiptoe to foresee the future," and cannot be happy until we "live with nature in the present, above time" (p. 151). Therefore we should always say "yes" to the present moment and surrender to what is, for what could be more insanely negative than to say no to life itself, which is always and ever *now*. A shift in consciousness from time to presence makes everything feel alive and emanates *being*. The eternal is timeless, not everlasting, and the infinite corresponds to the ground of our consciousness and being. It is not an object and it thus sizeless and formless, yet it embraces all forms and objects. When you come to know that *life*, not birth and death, is eternal, you will not be in any rush to experience as many sensations and things as possible within your seventy, eighty or more years, but you will appreciate them more keenly. Furthermore, when you *are* in your seventies, eighties, and beyond, you will appreciate them even *more* keenly.

Eternity is connected with the world of *being*, whereas time is connected with the world of *becoming*, where "nothing ever really is," according to Plato. In the outside world, there is a stream of becoming, while within there is a stream of ever-changing feelings and thoughts, in a succession of different "I"s or fragmentary bits of ourselves. It is an inner world of becoming in which nothing *is*, and in which we possess nothing lasting, including ourselves. These changing forms of inner and outer life led to the ancient Hindu concept of *Maya*, the belief that manifest being is somehow illusory, and that the way in which the world is experienced disguises the true unity of reality. This impermanence of forms as well as the changing cycles of life create much psychic suffering if we try to live by them. There is creation and destruction, birth and death, growth and dissolution, and inevitable cycles of gain and loss in the lives of individuals, as well as families, nations, and civilizations. Individually, our physical and psychic energy is subject to cycles and cannot always be at a peak. There will be times of high activity and creativity but also those of low activity and stagnation. This can be terribly demoralizing and much illness is created by fighting against the cycles of low energy, which are vital for regeneration. This needs to be known and accepted at the deepest level. We are not just *in* these cycles, we *are* them, and it all vibrates, oscillates, and goes around.

The perennial philosophy, originally coined *Philosophia Perennis* by Leibniz in the seventeenth century, has been described as a metaphysic that recognizes a divine Ground of Being. This Ground is ineffable in terms of discursive thought but open to being intuited by us in the world of things and lives. The ineffable intuition or illumination of the oneness that encompasses the multiplicity of all things is the source and ground of the philosophy. The experience or illumination of the oneness of the Ground is both immanent and transcendent, and in the aftermath of that experience one may recognize the cosmic significance of all life. Existence then becomes sacred and everything is affirmed just as it is, and that it has always been just right "such as it is." Even after the euphoria or transcendent nature of the experience evaporates, there is a sense of certainty and *acceptance* of the rightness of things that affects one's everyday life.

Speaking of the everyday brings back to mind the Eternal Now, in the sense that there seems to be a certain spiritual grandiosity to the term. Yet the closer one looks at it, the more it becomes apparent that we are *in* it every moment of every day. Because we are mentally caught in that flow of life called *time*, we feel we cannot arrest it or grasp it. But the reality is that we cannot get away from it. Try as we might to retain the past and hurry into the future, it is impossible to get out of the present moment. The more we try to grasp it, the more difficult it is to see that it holds us. This is simplicity itself and yet it is the Eternal Now in which many have said that God so lovingly holds us. Meister Eckhart (1924) claimed that the directness and simplicity of the presence of God in the now should enter and permeate our consciousness with ease. Knowing this, it should also be obvious that our everyday acts of sitting, walking, eating, washing, and working are done *in* God when done in a contemplative way. As he put it, "For in being, mere being, lies all that is all. Being is the first name . . . Our whole life ought to be being. So far as our life is being, so far it is in God" (Eckhart, 1924, p. 206). This is certainly one answer to the question in the title of this chapter, i.e., "Beyond Being?" Since being is *all*, the answer must be that there is nothing beyond it. This is so, certainly, from Eckhart's mystical and illuminating perspective.

That being is all is at the heart of the perennial philosophy, but is this more a faith than a philosophy? Let us put it this way, it is a *philosophical* faith in that it is not based on religious revelation. It is based on the fact that faith is deeply embedded in the human existential situation, as Karl Jaspers (1967) contended in *Philosophical Faith and Revelation.* But, then, can such a faith be a fiction, especially if it was enunciated by a mystic such as Eckhart? Wallace Stevens (1957, p. 163) might have had the last word on that when he wrote:

The final belief
Is to believe in a fiction
Which you know to be a fiction
There being nothing else
The exquisite truth is to know
That it is a fiction and that
You believe in it willingly.

James Hillman (1981) would not only agree but would claim that such a fiction is a "healing fiction." Yet at the contemplative level of aging, we are free to believe or not, for belief is not our destination but only a form of support along the way. And the *way* is simply being, which *has* been our destination all along. It is not in the future and it has never been in the past. It is always here and now. Thoreau, who did not live a long life by our standards, nevertheless got it right when he advised us to live each moment as it passes, "breathe the air, taste the fruit, and resign yourself to the influence of each." We can savor each experience, letting go and letting *be*. This *way of being* is as close as we can come to the ultimate *thing-in-itself.* It is all about process and not product, which brings us back to the original conundrum in Chapter One, of doing vs. being. In the final analysis, the being should be in the doing itself. Aristotle claimed that the goal of all action is contemplation. That might not be entirely the case, however, for much of the joy of being lies in the pleasure of doing. Yet this is doing of a different sort. It is doing something in the spirit of non-achievement, which has a good quality to it. Doing something simply for itself, in the free spirit of play, moves us beyond praise or blame and provides us with the detached interest of a newborn.

So contemplative aging is all about contemplating rather than its fruits, such as wisdom, although that is often a byproduct. Given the interiority of later life and the contemplative way of being, "the kingdom of heaven is within," as Jesus said. And that way of being is in the now: *Now*, when "the sea flows in our veins . . . and the stars are our jewels . . . when all things are infinite and holy" (Huxley, 1954). Beyond being? Why beyond, when we have the perennial present?

References

Ai, A. L., Park, C. L., & Shearer, M. (2007, November). Spiritual and religious involvement related to end-of-life decision-making in patients undergoing coronary bypass graft surgery. Paper presented at the annual meeting of the Gerontological Society of America, San Francisco.

Allport, G. (1950). *The individual and his religion: A psychological interpretation.* New York: Macmillan

Atchley, R. C. (2009). *Spirituality and aging.* Baltimore: Johns Hopkins University Press.

Atchley, R. C. (1999). *Continuity and adaptation in aging: Creating positive experiences*. Baltimore: Johns Hopkins University Press.

Atchley, R. C. (1997). Everyday mysticism: Spiritual development in later adulthood. *Journal of Adult Development*, 4(2), 123-134.

Bachelard, G. (1971). *The poetics of reverie: Childhood, language, and the cosmos* (D. Russell, Trans.) Boston: Beacon Press.

Bachelard, G. (1969). *The poetics of space.* (M. Jolas, Trans.) Boston: Beacon Press.

Baer, R. A. (Ed.). *2006). Mindfulness-based treatment approaches: Clinicians guide to evidence base and applications*. London: Academic Press.

Barrett, W. (Ed.). (1996). *Zen Buddhism: The selected writings of D. T. Suzuki*. New York: Doubleday Image.

Bateson, G. (1980). *Mind and nature: A necessary unity.* New York: E. P. Dutton.

Becker, E. (1973). *The denial of death*. New York: Free Press.

Bengtson, V. L. (1973). *The social psychology of aging*. Indianapolis: Boobs-Merrill.

Berenson, B. (1949). *Sketch for a self-portrait.* New York: Pantheon Books.

Berger, P. & Luckman, T. (1967). *The social construction of reality.* New York: Anchor.

Bergson, H. (1922). *Creative evolution* (A. Mitchell, Trans.). London: MacMillan.

Bienvenu, O. et al. (2007). Low extraversion and high neuroticism as indices of genetic and environmental risk for social phobia, agoraphobia, and animal phobia. *American Journal of Psychiatry, 164*, 1714-21.

Blake, W. (1994 [1790-93]). *Marriage of heaven and hell.* Mineola, NY: Dover Edition.

Boethius. (1962). *The consolation of philosophy* (R. Green, Trans.). New York: Macmillan.

Bolles, E. B. (1988). *Remembering and forgetting: Inquiries into the nature of memory*. New York: Walker & Co.

Boulding, K. E. (1987). *The image*. Ann Arbor: University of Michigan Press.

Braam, A. W., Bramsen, I., van Tilburg, T. G., van der Ploed, & Deeg, J. H. ((2006). Cosmic transcendence and framework of meaning in life: Patterns among older adults in the Netherlands, *The Journals of Gerontology Series B: Psychological Sciences and Social Sciences*, 61, S121-S128.

Bucke, M. A. (1923).*Cosmic consciousness*. New York: E. P. Dutton.

Butler, R. N. (1970). Looking forward to what? Life review, legacy and excessive identity versus change. *American Behavioral Scientist,* 14, 121-126.

Butler, R.N. (1963). The life review: An interpretation of reminiscence in the aged. *Psychiatry*, 26, 65-75.

Capra, F. (2001 [1975]). *The Tao of physics*: *An exploration of the parallels between modern physics and Eastern mysticism (25th anniversary edition)*. Boston, MA: *Shambhala Publications, Inc.*

Cassirer, E. (1944). *Essay on man*. New York: Doubleday.

Casey, E. S. (1997). *The fate of place: A philosophical history.* Berkeley: University of California Press.

Chaudhury, H. (2008). *Remembering home: Rediscovering the self in dementia.* Baltimore: The Johns Hopkins University Press.

Chaudhury, H. (2002). Journey back home: Recollecting past places by people with dementia. *Journal of Housing for the Elderly, 16*(1/2), 85-86.

Chaudhury, H. & Rowles, G. (2005). Between the shores of recollection and imagination: Self, aging and home. In Rowles, G. & Chaudhury, H. (Eds.), *Home and identity in late life: International perspectives.* New York: Springer.

Cicirelli, V. (2002). *Older adults views on death.* New York: Springer Publishing Company.

Cockerel, V. G. (2000). Older adults' ethnicity, fear of death, and end-of-life decisions. In A. Tomer (Ed.) *Death attitudes and the older adult.* Philadelphia: Brunner-Routledge.

Cockerel, V. (2002). *Older adult's views on death.* New York: Springer.

Cohen et al. (2005). Intrinsic and extrinsic religiosity, belief in the afterlife, death anxiety, and life satisfaction in young Catholics and Protestants. *Journal of Research in Personality, 39*(3), 307-324.

Cohler, Bertram J.(1992). The myth of successful aging. *The Gerontologist,* 32(1), 8-22.

Croce, B. (1965). *Guide to aesthetics*. (P. Romanell, Trans.). Indianapolis: Bobbs-Merrill.

Dalby, P. (2006). Is there a process of spiritual change or development associated with ageing? A critical review of research. *Aging & Mental Health, 10*(1), 4-12.

Damon, W., Lerner, R., & Eisenberg, N. (eds.) (2006). *Handbook of child psychology, vol. 3*. New York: Wiley.

Dearthage, G. (1979). The clinical use of 'mindfulness' meditation techniques in short-term therapy. In J. Welwood (Ed.), *The meeting of the ways*: *Explorations in east/west psychology*. (New York: Shocken Books.

Deikman, A. J. (1966). De-automatization and the mystic experience. *Psychiatry*, 29, 324-338.

Derrida, J. (1997). *Of Grammatology*. (G. C. Spivak, Trans.). Baltimore, MD: Johns Hopkins University Press.

Dewey, J. (1934). *Art as experience*. New York: G. P. Putnam.

Dewey, J. (1925). *Experience and nature*. Chicago: Open Court.

de Wit, H. F. (1991). *Contemplative psychology.* Pittsburgh: Duquesne University Press.

Duff, R. & Hong, L. (1995). Age density, religiosity, and death anxiety in retirement communities. *Review of Religious Research, 37*(1), 19-32.

Earle, W. (1972). *The autobiographical consciousness.* Chicago: Quadrangle Books.

Eckhart, Meister (1998). In R. Van de Weyer (Ed.). *Eckhart: Philosophers of the spirit*. London: Hodder & Stoughton.

Eckhart, Meister (1924). *Works.* (C. B. Evans, Trans.). London: John M. Watkins.

Edelman, G. M. (1989). *The remembered present: A biological theory of consciousness*. New York: Basic Books.

Emerson, R. W. (1981). Self-reliance. In *The Portable Emerson*. (C. Bode & M. Cowley, Eds.). New York: Penguin Books.

Emerson, R. W. (1870). *Society and solitude*. Boston: Fields, Osgood & Co.

Emerson, R. W. (1990). Terminus. In R. D. Richardson (Ed.). *Selected essays, lectures, and poems.* New York: Bantam.

Epicurus (1995). In P. Hadot. *Philosophy as a way of life.* Malden, MA: Blackwell.

Erikson, E. H. (1968). *Childhood and society, 2nd Ed.* New York: Norton.

Erikson, E. H. (1982). *The life cycle completed*. New York: Norton.

Erikson, E. H. (1986). *Vital involvement in old age*. New York: Norton.

Eysenck's personality inventory and the four temperaments. (2010). http://www.odportal.com/personality/eysenck.htm

Eysenck, H. J. & Eysenck, M. W. (1985). *Personality and individual differences: A natural science approach.* New York: Plenum Press.

Farber, S. (1981). *Identical twins reared apart: A reanalysis.* New York: Basic Books.

Feifel, H. (Ed.) (1959). *The meaning of death.* New York: McGraw-Hill.

Fingarette, H. (1996). *Death: Philosophical soundings*. Chicago: Open Court.

Fortner, B. V. & Niemeyer, R. A. (1999). Death anxiety in older adults: A quantitative review. *Death Studies, 23*, 387-411.

Freud, S. (1958). Death instinct. In H. B. English & A. C. English (Eds.). *A comprehensive dictionary of psychological and psychoanalytical terms*. New York: David McKay, Inc.

Freud, S. (1995). *The basic writings of Sigmund Freud* (A. A. Brill, Ed.). New York: Modern Library.

Fromm, E. (1941). *Escape from freedom*. New York: Holt, Rinehart, & Winston.

Fromm, E. (1992). *The art of being.* New York: Continuum.

Fromm, E. (1976). *To have or to be*. New York: Harper & Row, 1976.

Germer, C. K., Siegel, R. D., & Fulton, P. R. (2005). *Mindfulness and psychotherapy*. New York: Guilford.

Gutmann, D. L. (1974). Alternatives to disengagement: The old men of the Highland Druze. In R. LeVine (Ed.), *Culture and personality: Contemporary readings.* Chicago: Aldine.

Gutmann, D. L. (1964). An exploration of ego configurations in middle and later life. In B. L. Neugarten (Ed.), *Personality in middle and later life.* New York: Atherton.

Hadot, P. (1995). *Philosophy as a way of life*. (A. I. Davidson, Ed.; M. Chase, Trans.) Malden, MA: Blackwell.

Hadot, P. *Plotinus or the simplicity of vision.* (1993). (M. Chase, Trans.) Chicago: University of Chicago Press.

Hanh, T. N. (1996). *Breathe! You are alive.* Berkeley, CA: Parallax.

Hanh, T. N. (1975). *The miracle of mindfulness: A manual on meditation.* Boston: Beacon.

Hayes, S. C., Follette, V. M., & Linehan, M. M. (Eds.), *Mindfulness and acceptance: Expanding the cognitive-behavioral tradition.* New York: Guilford, 2004.

Heidegger, M. (1962). *Being and time*. (J. Macquarrie & E. Robinson, Trans.) New York: Harper & Row.

Heraclitus (1994). Heraclitus of Ephesus. In R. D. McKirahan (Ed.). *Philosophy before Socrates.* Indianapolis: Hackett Publishing.

Herman, J. B. (1996). *I and Tao: Martin Buber's encounter with Chuang Tzu*. Albany: State University of New York Press.

Hillman, J. (1999). *The force of character and the lasting life.* New York: Random House.

Hillman, J. (1996). *The soul's code: In search of character and calling.* New York: Random House.

Hoelter, J. W. (1979). Multidimensional treatment of fear of death. *Journal of Consulting and Clinical Psychology*, 47, 996-999.

Hood, R. W. & Morris, R. J. (1983). Toward a theory of death transcendence. *Journal for the Scientific Study of Religion, 22*, 353-365.

Husserl, E. (1999). *The idea of phenomenology.* (L. Hardy, Trans.). Boston: Kluwer Academic.

Huxley, A. (1954). *The doors of perception.* New York: Harper & Brothers.

James, W. (1996). *A pluralistic universe*. Lincoln, NE: University of Nebraska Press.

James, W. (1950). *The principles of psychology*. (Vol.1). New York: Dover Publications.

James, W. (1985). *Psychology: The briefer course*. Notre Dame, IN: University of Notre Dame Press.

James, W. (1961). *The varieties of religious experience*. New York: Collier Books.

James, W. (1956). *The will to believe*. New York: Dover Publications.

Jaspers, K. (1967). *Philosophical faith and revelation*. New York: Harper & Row.

Jaspers, K. (1971). *Philosophy* (3 Vols.). Chicago: University of Chicago Press.

Jung, C. G. (2009). *The red book*. New York. W. W. Norton.

Jung, C. G. (1965). *Memories, dreams, reflections*. New York: Vantage

Jung, C. G. (1959). The soul and death. In H. Feifel (Ed.). *The meaning of death*. New York: McGraw-Hill.

Kagan, J. (1994). *Galen's prophecy: Temperament in human nature*. New York: Basic Books.

Katz, R. K. (1990). *The problem of pure consciousness: Mysticism and philosophy*. New York: Oxford.

Kundera, M. (1984). *The unbearable lightness of being*. New York: Harper & Row.

Learning Theories.com: Constructivism. (2010). http://www.learning-theories.com/constructivism.html

Levinson, M., Jennings, P., Aldwin, C., & Shiraishi, R. (2005). Self-transcendence: Conceptualization and measurement. *The International Journal of Aging and Human Development, 60*(2), 127-143.

Lewin, F. & Thomas, L. (2001). Gerotranscendence and life satisfaction: Studies of religious and secular Iranians and Turks. *Journal of Religious Gerontology, 12*(1), 17-41.

Lifton, R. J. (1979). *The broken connection: On death and the continuity of life*. New York: Simon & Schuster.

Lifton, R. J. (1976). *The life of the self.* New York: Basic Books.

MCTFR: Minnesota Center for Twin and Family Research (2010). http://mctfr.psych.umn.edu/

Mann, T. (1995). *The magic mountain*. (J. E. Woods, Trans.). New York: Vintage.

May, G. G. (1982). *Will and spirit: A contemplative psychology.* San Francisco: Harper & Row.

McCrae, R. et al. (2000). Nature over nurture: Temperament, personality, and life span development. *Journal of Personality and Social Psychology, 78*(1), 173-86.

Montaigne, M. (1992). *The complete essays.* (M. A. Screech, Trans.). New York: Viking Penguin.

Montaigne, M. (1952). *The essays of Michel Eyquem de Montaigne.* (W. C. Hazlitt, Ed.; C. Cotton, Trans.). Chicago: Encyclopaedia Britannica Great Books Edition.

Mysteries of twins, the. (1998). *The Washington Post,* Sunday, January 11.

Neugarten, B. L. (Ed.) (1968). *Middle age and aging.* Chicago: University of Chicago Press.

Neugarten, B. L. (1973). Personality change in later life: A developmental perspective. In *The psychology of adult development and aging.* Washington, DC: American Psychological Association.

Neugarten, B. L, Havighurst, R., & Tobin S. (1961). Life Satisfaction Index [LSI]. *Clinical and Social Psychology, 6,* 219-222, 237-239.

Niemeyer, R. A. & Van Brunt, D. (1995). Death anxiety. In H. Wass, F. M. Berardo, & R. A. Niemeyer (Eds.). *Dying: Facing the facts* (3rd Ed.) (pp. 49-88). Washington DC: Hemisphere.

Peck, R. C. (1968). Psychological developments in the second half of life. In B. L. Neugarten (Ed.), *Middle age and aging.* Chicago: University of Chicago Press.

Pieper, J. (1958). *Happiness and contemplation.* (R. Winston and C. Winston, Trans.). New York: Pantheon Books.

Pieper, J. (1963). *Leisure: The basis of culture.* (G. Malsbary, Trans.). New York: Pantheon Books.

Pinker, S. (2002). *The blank slate: The modern denial of human nature.* New York: Penguin Books.

Plotinus. (1993). In P. Hadot, *Plotinus or the simplicity of vision.* (M. Chase, Trans.) Chicago: University of Chicago Press.

Progoff, I. (1975). *At a journal workshop: The basic text and guide for using the intensive journal process.* New York: Dialogue House.

Progoff, I. (1957). *The cloud of unknowing.* New York: The Julian Press.

Progoff, I. (1980). *The practice of process meditation.* New York: Dialogue House.

Proust, M. (1948). *Aphorisms and epigrams from remembrance of things past.* (J. O'Brien, Trans.). New York: McGraw-Hill.

Proust, M. (1981). *Remembrance of things past.* (C. K. Scott-Moncrieff & T. Kilmartin, Trans.) New York: Random House.

Ram Dass (2000). *Still here: Embracing aging, changing, and dying.* New York: Riverhead Books.

Randall, W. S. (1998). *George Washington: A life.* New York: Henry Holt & Co.

Rilke, R. M. (2006). *Letters on life.* (U. Baer, Trans.). New York: Modern Library.

Rilke, R. M. (1984). *Letters to a young poet.* (S. Mitchell, Trans.). New York: Random House.

Romaniuk, M. & Romaniuk, J. G. (1981). Looking back: An analysis of reminiscence functions and triggers," *Experimental Aging Research,* 81, 477-481.

Rousseau, J. (1979). *Reveries of the solitary walker.* (P. France, Trans.). New York: Viking Penguin.

Salam, A. & Wigner, E. (Eds.) (2009). *Aspects of quantum theory.* Cambridge: Cambridge University Press.

Sartre, J. P. (1966). *Being and nothingness.* (H. E. Barnes, Trans.). New York: Washington Square Press.

Sartre, J. P. (1993). *The family idiot: Gustave Flaubert.* (C. Cosman, Trans.). Chicago: The University of Chicago Press.

Scarr, S. (1969). Social introversion—extraversion as a heritable response. *Child Development, 40*(3), 823-832.

Schopenhauer, A. (1969). *The World as will and representation* (2 Vols.). New York: Dover.

Schweitzer, A. (1947). *Albert Schweitzer: An anthology.* (A. C. Joy, Ed.). Boston: Beacon Press.

Scott-Maxwell, F. (1979). *Measure my days.* New York: Penguin Books.

Semrad, E. V. (1960). *Teaching psychotherapy of psychotic patients.* New York: Grune & Stratton.

Sherman, E. (2008, October). Attitudes concerning death and symbolic immortality among the elderly: A phenomenological study. Paper presented at the annual program meeting of the Society for Phenomenology and the Human Sciences, Pittsburgh.

Sherman, E. (1991). *Reminiscence and the self in old age*. New York: Springer Publishing Company.

Sherman, E. (1985). Social reconstruction variables and the morale of the aged. *Journal of Aging and Human Development*, 20, 133-144.

Sherman, E. & Siporin, M. (2008). Contemplative theory and practice for social work. *Journal of Religion and Spirituality in Social Work*, 27, 259-274.

Sherman, E., and Webb, T. A. (1994). The self as process in late-life reminiscence, *Ageing and Society*, *Vol.14*, (No. 2), 255-267.

Sherman, E., & Peak, T. (1991). Patterns of reminiscence and the assessment of late life adjustment. *Gerontological Social Work*, 16, 59-74.

Sigelman, C. & Rider, E. (2008). *Life-span human development*. Sixth Edition. Belmont, CA: Wadsworth Cengage Learning.

Singh, A. & Misra, N. (2009). Loneliness, depression, and sociability in old age. *Industrial Psychiatry Journal, 18*(1), 51-55.

Stace, W. T. (1961). *Mysticism and philosophy.* London: Macmillan.

Stace, W. T. (1960). *The teaching of the mystics*. New York: The New American Library.

Storr, A. (1983). *The essential Jung*. Princeton, NJ: Princeton University Press.

Suzuki, D. T. (1979). *Mysticism: Christian and Buddhist*. London: George Allen & Unwin.

Suzuki, D. T. (1956). The doctrine of no-mind. In W. Barrett (Ed.) *Zen Buddhism: Selected writings of D. T. Suzuki.* New York: Doubleday.

Thoreau, H. D. (1999). *Walden and civil disobedience.* New York: Signet Classic.

Thorson, J. A., & Powell, F. C. (1990). Meanings of death and intrinsic religiosity. *Journal of Clinical Psychology, 46,* 379-391.

Tillich, P. (1973). *Systematic theology, vol. 1.* Chicago: University of Chicago Press.

Tillich, P. (1963). *The eternal now*. New York: Scribner.

Tillich, P. (1955). *The new being.* New York: Scribner.

Tillich, P. (1952). *The courage to be*. New Haven: Yale University Press.

Tomer, A. (2000). *Death attitudes and the older adult.* Philadelphia: Brunner-Routledge.

Tornstam, L. (2005). *Gerotranscendence: A developmental theory of positive aging.* New York: Springer Publishing Company.

Tornstam, L. (1997). Gerotranscendence: The contemplative dimension of aging. *Journal of Aging Studies, 11*(2), 143-154.

Turunen, M. (2008). Trends in temperament research. *Acta Paediatrica, 77*(s344), 81-86.

Vandecreek, L., & Nye, C. (1993). Testing the death transcendence scale. *Journal for the Scientific Study of Religion, 32*, 279-283.

Van de Weyer, R. (Ed.). (1998). *Eckhart.* London: Hodder & Stoughton.

Watts, A. W. (1975). *Tao: The watercourse way.* New York: Pantheon Books.

Watts, A. W. (1966). *The book.* New York: Collier Books.

Watzlawick, P. (Ed.). (1984). *The invented reality.* New York: Norton.

Waxman, B. F. (1999). Nature, spirituality, and later life in literature: An essay on the romanticism of older writers. *The Gerontologist*, 39, 516-524.

Whitehead, A. N. (1920). *The concept of nature.* Cambridge: Cambridge University Press.

Whitehead, A. N. (1929). *Process and reality: An essay in cosmology.* New York: Macmillan.

Whitehead, A. N. (1967). *Science and the modern world.* New York: Macmillan.

Whorf, B. J. (1956). *Language, thought, and reality.* J. B. Carroll (Ed.). Cambridge, MA: MIT Press.

Wilson, R. & Matheny, A. (1983). Assessment of temperament in infant twins. *Developmental Psychology, 19*(2), 172-183.

Wink, P. & Dillon, M. (2002). Spiritual development across the adult life course: Findings from a longitudinal study. *Journal of Adult Development, 9*(1), 79-94.

Wink, P. & Scott, J. (2005). Does religiousness buffer against the fear of death and dying in late adulthood? Findings from a longitudinal study. *The Journals of Gerontology: Series B, 60*(4), 207-214.

Wittkowski, J. (1988). Relationships between religiosity and attitudes toward death and dying in a middle-aged sample. *Personality and Individual Differences*, *9*, 307-312.

Yutang, L. (2001 [1937]). *The importance of living.* Singapore: Cultured Lotus.

Zukav, G. (2001). *Dancing Wu Li masters. An overview of the New Physics.* New York: HarperOne.

Index

Sept 2017 - MaryAnn Needham TODAY IS 8/18/18

BOB's emergency - health - fear - husband

Taxi ride - N.J.

Terry - CA - friend

TERRY - move - friend

Elaine - move - friend

70 yrs old - my health -

Gary's - death - brother - only

Mel's death - uncle - last of father's siblings

Norma's death - aunt - last of mother's siblings

Christian's farewell - "son"

Jon & Dan - more distance - nephews

Carol - more distance - niece

Carrie - more distance - stepdaughter

Carol Beeners - move - Spiritual Counselor

RETIREMENT - "ego" - purpose

CPSIA information can be obtained
at www.ICGtesting.com
Printed in the USA
LVOW03s0043221117
557265LV00001B/109/P

9 781884 09299